What people are saying about . . .

a lifelong love

"If you enjoyed the acclaimed and bestselling *Sacred Marriage* by Gary Thomas, you've got to read *A Lifelong Love*. This book is incredible. Consider it your road map to obtaining all that God designed your marriage to be. You absolutely don't want to miss out on this life-changing message."

Drs. Les and Leslie Parrott, authors of
Saving Your Marriage Before It Starts

"When Gary Thomas writes anything, I pay attention. When he writes about relationships or family, I pay more attention. When he writes about marriage, I pay attention in the fullest way possible. He has a rare gift to take what we may think we know, and turn it inside out for a fresh reexamination using Scripture. Marriage is the most important relationship we have apart from the one we have with God. I am thankful for Gary's passion and commitment to help us experience growth, no matter if we're newly married or married many years. This is yet another Gary Thomas book I will recommend and use both personally and as a pastor in our church."

Dan Kimball, pastor and author of
How (Not) to Read the Bible

"*A Lifelong Love* is a powerful reminder that marriage is more than just a social construct or a legal arrangement. It is a deeply spiritual act ordained by God Himself. I believe married couples will find it practical and inspiring as they pursue deeper intimacy in their relationships."

Jim Daly, president of Focus on the Family

"A profound, beautiful, and lifelong love in marriage is anchored in our relationship with God. This book takes you there!"

Dr. Tim Clinton, president of the American Association of Christian Counselors

"Gary Thomas has done it again. *A Lifelong Love* is another timely, well-crafted book for every married couple. Gary's words carry some needed encouragement, instruction, and hope. This is not just another marriage book; it lifts marriage back to the noble place where it belongs … one of transcendent and magnificent glory."

Dr. Dennis Rainey, host of *FamilyLife Today*

"There are so many marriage books out there, but in my mind, Gary Thomas is like the Good Housekeeping Seal of Approval. I've thoroughly enjoyed so many of his works through the years, such as *Sacred Marriage* and *Pure Pleasure*, and I am thrilled that he's contributed yet another marriage-building, affair-proofing, family-strengthening, God-honoring book to guide those of us who take marriage very seriously!"

Shannon Ethridge, author of the bestselling Every Woman's Battle series and *The Passion Principles*

"Gary Thomas has written another deep and powerful book full of biblical wisdom and practical suggestions for a loving, lifelong marriage that is more than simply staying together, precisely because it is God-centered and empowered by the Holy Spirit. A must-read for every married couple!"

Dr. Siang-Yang Tan, professor of psychology at
Fuller Theological Seminary and senior pastor
of First Evangelical Church in Glendale, CA

"No other author I'm aware of offers such a spiritually rich framework for understanding and thriving in marriage. In *A Lifelong Love*, Gary Thomas powerfully cuts through all the hype to offer us real hope for a healthy marriage grounded in God. This is a deep, satisfying book that will lead you to the path of true joy in marriage."

Jud Wilhite, senior pastor of Central Christian
Church in Las Vegas and author of *Pursued*

"This book is like *Sacred Marriage*, Part 2. Gary shows you how to practically live out your marriage with an eternal perspective. *A Lifelong Love* teaches the paradox of letting go of happiness and finding hope and mission in the process. Regardless of the state of your marriage, this book will challenge and encourage you!"

Dr. Juli Slattery, psychologist and
cofounder of Authentic Intimacy

"Many marriage books focus on skills, but this book builds skills on deep theology. I love Gary's reflective writing style. This book demands a sermon series, and our church will be one of the first to use it."

Ted Cunningham, pastor of Woodland
Hills Family Church and author of *A
Love That Laughs* and *Fun Loving You*

a
lifelong
love

UPDATED & REVISED

BESTSELLING AUTHOR OF *SACRED MARRIAGE*

GARY THOMAS

a lifelong love

Discovering How Intimacy *with* God
Breathes Passion *into* Your Marriage

DAVID C COOK

transforming lives together

A LIFELONG LOVE
Published by David C Cook
4050 Lee Vance Drive
Colorado Springs, CO 80918 U.S.A.

Integrity Music Limited, a Division of David C Cook
Brighton, East Sussex BN1 2RE, England

The graphic circle C logo is a registered trademark of David C Cook.

The author has changed some names and details of
testimonies in this book for the sake of privacy.

The author has added italics to Scripture quotations for emphasis.

Library of Congress Control Number 2015936911
ISBN 978-0-8307-8120-1
eISBN 978-0-8307-8121-8

© 2014, 2021 Gary Thomas
Published in association with Yates & Yates, www.yates.com.
Previously published as *A Lifelong Love: How to Have Intimacy, Friendship, and
Purpose in Your Marriage* in 2014 © Gary Thomas, ISBN 978-1-4347-0862-5

The Team: Michael Covington, Stephanie Bennett, David Webb,
Judy Gillispie, James Hershberger, Susan Murdock
Cover Design: James Hershberger

Printed in the United States of America
Second Edition 2021

2 3 4 5 6 7 8 9 10 11

040521-KEP

*This book is dedicated in celebration of my son
Graham's marriage to Molly on July 12, 2014.*

*May you both grow in grace and love for each
other as you enjoy the blessing of a lifelong love.*

Contents

.

Acknowledgments

I am indebted to so many individuals who graciously provided their time, wisdom, and constructive comments during early drafts of this book: Karen Lee-Thorp, first edition, and David Webb, who helped me edit the focus on this second edition; Drs. Steve and Rebecca Wilke; Alfonso Gilbert; Dr. Melody Rhode; Mary Kay Smith; Mike Salisbury; Lisa Thomas; Dr. Gerrit Dawson; Dr. Mitch Whitman; Jeff and Cheryl Scruggs; Dr. Juli Slattery; Alli Smith; Toni Richmond; Brooks Powell; and John Stanley. I am further indebted to the congregation of Second Baptist Church, Houston, Texas, under the leadership of Dr. Ed Young and Ben Young, for their generosity in keeping me on as writer-in-residence.

I can't imagine writing without my agents, Curtis Yates and Mike Salisbury. I am also very grateful for my friends at David C Cook—Michael Covington, Stephanie Bennett, David Webb, Judy Gillispie, Nathan Landry, and others.

There is, of course, one person who could single-handedly torpedo or bless my life and ministry, and that's Lisa Thomas, my wife of thirty-six years as of June 3, 2020. She has lived this life and this truth with me, making it a delight and a joy to explore the reaches of worship and intimacy in marriage. Lisa, we began walking the journey of a lifelong love in 1984, and I'm *still* eager to see where it leads.

It's What You Do with It

I have loved you with an everlasting love;
Therefore I have drawn you out with kindness.
I will build you again and you will be rebuilt.

—Jeremiah 31:3-4 NASB

When German-speaking Mennonites began migrating to the Central American nation of Belize in the 1950s, Belizean officials were a bit wary. It had been barely a decade since World War II, and though the Mennonites didn't look, act, or talk like Nazis, they *spoke* German, and so, despite the fact they had been living in Mexico since the 1920s, they were suspect. What to do?

The Mennonites wanted nothing more than to be free to practice their religion, teach their children in their own schools in their own language, be exempt from military service (they were pacifists), and set up their own farming community. In the end, the Belizean government permitted them to immigrate but gave them the most unproductive land in the country, the property no one else wanted.

It was a brilliant solution, though perhaps not in the way the Belizean officials anticipated. By applying their committed faith and work ethic, the Mennonites eventually made their part of Belize not just productive and fruitful but, indeed, *the most fruitful and productive region of the entire country.* Today, the Belizean Mennonites produce a large portion of the country's agricultural output—including 85 percent of all poultry and dairy products—from land that, a hundred years ago, nobody else wanted![1]

"You know as soon as you hit the Mennonite area," a person from Belize once said to me. "You just know."

It's an inspiring tale and not a bad picture of what can be made of a marriage. It is possible, with faith and effort, to begin with a relationship that is unproductive and perhaps even unwanted and end up spiritually feeding others from its fruits.

Maybe you feel like you have nothing left to give to your marriage. Perhaps it's difficult to even imagine that your relationship could be satisfying, much less inspiring to others. You may feel, as many do, that your marriage is stuck in a rut that grows deeper by the day or that you and your spouse lack the raw materials or "natural resources" of compatibility to ever achieve anything even resembling happiness.

Is it possible that a relationship like yours could become a source of profound joy, rich togetherness, and powerful witness? You may have dreamed of an intimate, lifelong love but now wonder if you can make it to the end of this *year* without losing your mind to boredom, frustration, or animosity.

Or maybe you're actually in a *good* place in your relationship but you're wondering if you've got what it takes to make it last. You've seen so many couples start out well and end miserably, and you don't want that.

How do I know all this? I've met you! I've received countless emails, sat down with many people just like you, and faced plenty of challenging seasons in my own thirty-plus years of marriage. One thing three decades of marriage—as well as counseling married couples as a pastor in the nation's fourth-largest city—gives you is a realistic understand-ing of just how difficult marriage can be at times. Marriage has such amazing potential and can often be a rich, joyous, and life-giving rela-tionship. But sometimes it can seem as though it's sucking the very life out of you. And the bounce between these two extremes can happen faster than it takes an ice cream cone to melt in August.

The spiritual principle we can take from Belize and that gives us hope as we look forward to building a lifelong love is this: *it's not what you have; it's what you do with it.* When God becomes part of the equation, it's not what we bring into our marriages, what we can learn, or what we can figure out on our own. It's what we do with His empowering presence that lays the foundation for an ever-deepening intimacy and a beautiful, satisfying relationship.

The prophet Jeremiah proclaimed a bold promise from God to His people:

> I have loved you with an everlasting love;
> Therefore I have drawn you out with kindness.
> I will build you again and you will be rebuilt.
> (Jer. 31:3–4 NASB)

Time and time again I have seen the dynamic in this passage manifested in my own marriage. (I realize it is poor scriptural inter-pretation to take a promise made to the Israelites and arbitrarily apply it to marriage. I am not intending to proof-text here, but rather using biblical language to paint for you a picture, each element of which *will* be supported with appropriately applied scriptures later in the text.)

Like you, I have been discouraged at times, recognizing that my wife and I have fallen into the same old rut, occasionally even wondering if perhaps we just weren't a "good match." I want as much as anybody to experience a *lifelong* love. I don't want a marriage that limps to the finish line. I yearn to see renewed affection, to rekindle passion, and to share a deeper intimacy through the years. And three big spiritual truths with a lot of little implications have given me a glimpse of a new way forward.

Here's what I have found and am continually finding—that for two sinners to grow in affection for each other even as they learn more about each other requires more than a few romantic gimmicks and marital tricks to pull it off. Experiencing a lifelong love requires that both husband and wife have:

1. **A "magnificent obsession" with God and His kingdom.** This will give us the motivation to love each other in the face of repeated disappointment. This obsession enriches and gives meaning to our lives, which in turn enriches and gives meaning to our marriages. Profoundly so. This is about *spiritual intimacy.*

2. **A passion to fight normal marital drift by intentionally growing together.** In a world that seems bent on pulling us apart, we must be thoughtful and purposeful in growing together. This is about *relational intimacy.*

3. **A new understanding of love *as God defines it.*** Marriage is frustrating when we live with an agenda that is different from God's. If we don't learn and embrace what love is from God's perspective, we will resent what God created marriage to celebrate and showcase. This is about *devotional intimacy.*

Think of these three elements—a magnificent obsession with God, a passionate pursuit of relational intimacy, and a new understanding of love—as three legs of a stool. Together, they provide a sturdy foundation to support a lifelong love. If you take away just one of these legs—for example, focusing on God and love but not intentionally growing together—the stool will be unbalanced and your relationship headed for a fall. Likewise, if you focus on love and an intimate union but ignore God, you will eventually lose your way and the relationship will come crashing down.

The point of this three-point approach is to acknowledge the triune God as the center, the model, and the empowering agent of our marriages. *He* sets the agenda for what we should desire, what we should strive for, and how we can get there. He even promises to make it happen: "I will build you again and you will be rebuilt." This makes the meaning of our marriages something much bigger and grander than we ever could have dreamed.

What is the situation in your marriage as you begin this undertaking? This approach will address virtually any season or condition of marriage:

- people who are frustrated with the person they married and who wonder how they can find fulfillment in the midst of it,
- those who believe they've made generally good choices but whose marriage hasn't lived up to all they hoped it might be, or
- those who simply desire to take their marriage to new levels by bolstering it with a spiritual purpose and dynamic that has been lacking up till now.

Here's the question we seek to answer: How can we remake our marriages to become fruitful relationships that breathe spiritual life, that create intimate union, that enable us to grow together through the years, and that God can use to encourage others?

Let's begin with what I like to call the magnificent obsession.

Part 1

The Magnificent Obsession

Worshipping Our Way to Happiness

God knows you didn't marry someone who is always easy to love. In fact, His Word proclaims that you've married someone who will stumble in *many* ways (James 3:2).

He gets that marriage isn't always easy. He knows you will be tried and tested. If you're in one of those seasons of marriage where this is proving to be true, don't freak out. He's got this. But His remedy *isn't* to make your spouse perfect. His plan is to help *you* learn to love an imperfect person out of reverence for a perfect God.

I learned this the hard way as a young husband, via a prayer that left me gloriously ruined. It came almost as a warning and, frankly, I needed one at the time. During an intense time of prayer, I sensed God telling me very directly that Lisa wasn't just my wife. She was also His *daughter*, and I was to treat her accordingly.

It was an intense application of 1 John 3:1: "See what kind of love the Father has given to us, that we should be called children of God" (ESV).

This was a moment of revelation for me, and the force of this insight grew once I had kids of my own. If you want to get on my good side, just be kind to one of my kids. A wonderful young woman at our church became Allison's "big sister" when my daughter was in her early teens, taking Ally out for coffee or ice cream and being an overall positive influence. My wife and I will love Amy the rest of our lives for the way she was so generous to one of our children.

Conversely, if you really want to make me angry, pick on my kids. Be mean to them, and my blood pressure will spike if your name is even mentioned. I'd much rather you mess with me than with my kids.

So when I realized I was married to *God's* daughter—and that women are married to God's sons—everything about how I viewed marriage changed. God feels about my wife, His daughter, in an even holier and more passionate way than I feel about my own daughters. Suddenly, my marriage was no longer about just me and one other person; it was very much a relationship with a passionately interested third partner. I realized that one of my primary forms of worship throughout the rest of my life would be honoring God by taking care of a woman who would always be, to His mind, "His little girl."

John's word that we are called children of God goes for all believers. So when we get married, God becomes even more to us than a Father—He is also our Father-in-Law. How can He be *both*? In the same way Jesus is simultaneously our brother, our Savior, our King, and our God.

When I disrespect my wife or am condescending toward her or mistreat her in any way, I am courting trouble with her heavenly Father, who feels passionately about her welfare. "Remember that the heavenly Father to whom you pray has no favorites. He will judge or reward you according to what you do. So you must live in reverent fear of him during your time here as 'temporary residents'" (1 Pet. 1:17 NLT).

In a positive sense, when I am actively caring for my wife, loving her, and seeking opportunities to showcase her beautiful qualities to others, I am pleasing God on about as high a level as He can be pleased.

"She's Going to Be Okay"

My earthly father-in-law, Bill, had been battling leukemia for seven years. He was ready to go home with the Lord, and over the phone he asked me to pray that God would let him go home *that day*.

My thoughts went back to our wedding rehearsal dinner, when Bill broke into tears telling me how happy he was about the next day's wedding. Bill wasn't a particularly sentimental guy, and almost two decades passed before he explained what was behind the tears that day: "Gary, when you married my daughter, I thought to myself, *I don't have to worry about Lisa. She's found a guy who will take care of her. She's going to be okay.*"

Now that I have two adult daughters, I can empathize. And so, during our final conversation, after we mutually shared some personal things, I told Bill, "I just want you to know how grateful I am that you gave me Lisa, and I want to remind you that you don't ever have to worry about Lisa. I'll make sure she's okay."

He said, "I know you will, Gary. I know you will."

I said what I did because I could imagine that on my own deathbed, that would be exactly what I would want to hear. Secure about my eternal destiny (as Bill was about his), I'd be most concerned about those I was leaving behind. I'd want to know someone would be there for my daughters.

That day reminded me that the best gift I can give a father-in-law is to take care of and cherish his beloved daughter. Seeing

God as my Father-in-Law has helped me to understand the apostle Peter's words when he wrote:

> Husbands, in the same way be considerate as you live with your wives, and treat them with respect ... so that nothing will hinder your prayers. (1 Pet. 3:7)

That used to seem backwards to me. I thought I needed to pray for a better marriage, but Peter was telling me I need a better marriage so I can pray. Thinking of God as my Father-in-Law resolved the dilemma.

If a young man came to me, praising me, complimenting me on my character, even singing songs about me and giving me ten percent of his income, and all the while I knew he was making one of my daughters miserable through abuse or neglect, I'd frankly have nothing to say to him except, "Hey, buddy, start treating my daughter better, and then we can talk. You say you respect me? Then take care of my cherished daughter." That would be the first and only thing I'd want to discuss with him every time he approached me. So it makes total sense that if I don't treat Lisa well, respecting her as God's daughter, with all the privileges such a high standing involves, my prayer life will be hindered.

I met a young woman who was raised by a single mom and who married into an extremely wealthy family. The family's wedding present to her was to pay off her considerable student loan and credit card debt—and then they bought a house for her mom! She asked me, "How can I ever repay them?"

My answer was simple: "Love their son as a husband has never been loved. There are few parents alive who wouldn't give most of what they have to see their children loved so well by their spouses."

I can never begin to repay God for what He has done for me. But I can love His daughter well. I can make Him smile by how I treat her. And one of His smiles is worth more to me than anything else in this world.

When I become obsessed with worshipping and thanking a perfect God who has treated me so well, loving an imperfect child of His feels like such a small thing in comparison.

Imagine Your Son

Anna, a mother of five children all under eight years of age, is understandably tired. It's impossible *not* to be tired if you have five kids that young. She's married to Michael, a rising lawyer and almost-certain future partner of a prestigious law firm. The problem Anna wants resolved is a common one: Michael has a high sex drive, and Anna has almost none.

She's understandably concerned that as Michael's star rises at work, particularly with younger associates and interns, he could be targeted for sexual temptation. But she's not concerned enough to have sex nearly as often as Michael would like.

"What do you think would make Michael happy?" I asked.

"He told me he'd be happy with two times a week, ecstatic with three."

"As opposed to the current …"

"Maybe once a month, if I'm honest."

"Maybe once a month" virtually qualifies as a "sexless marriage." A definition accepted by most marital therapists is ten times a year or less.

There were extenuating circumstances that we talked about, and things I could and did say later to Michael. (Talking about "obligation sex" never works long-term, so I'd never approach a situation like this from that motivation.)

But the image that Anna later told me most opened her eyes was this: I asked her to imagine her oldest son all grown up, married, and with small kids. He works a busy job and travels a fair amount. His vocation requires him to be around young, energetic women, and he's a star in their galaxy. He also happens to have a high sex drive.

"Okaaaay ...," Anna said.

"You want your son to be a faithful husband and a man of integrity, right?"

"Of course."

"And because you raised him right, he's doing his best. But I want you to consider this: If your future daughter-in-law treated him like you're treating Michael right now, would you be frustrated with her or grateful to her?"

Anna was silent for a long while. Her voice dropped two levels of softness when she finally replied, "Well, I wouldn't be happy with her."

Women, to quickly get a feel for how well you're treating your husband—God's son—consider how you'd feel if a daughter-in-law treated your boy the way you treat your husband, in any area. Would you thank God for her? Or would you be pleading with God to convict her spirit and soften her heart?

You see, worshipping God as our Father-in-Law helps prevent the scourge of so many marriages: taking our spouses for granted. This change in perspective will also encourage us to stop being "prosecuting attornies" and to start living as our spouses' "defense counselors."

This was revolutionary for me!

From Prosecuting Attorney to Defense Counselor

The vicar in a small British village had heard enough. Jean had visited him once too often and always with the same complaint. The clergyman's patience was at an end, so he said to Jean, "You've been coming here now for seven weeks. All I've been hearing is continual carping about how awful it has been for you being married to Reg, how mean and bad-tempered he is. I'm fed up with hearing the same old thing week in and week out. I don't want to hear any more. Before we go on, I want you to go into the church and ask God to show you just what life must have been like for Reg all these years and why he's become as he is."

Jean was dumbfounded. How could a man who called himself a priest be so unchristian and insensitive? Of course, he was a man— men do stick together. He probably thought it was the woman's fault, as always!

But then Jean went into the church to pray.

At first, she recited to God all the good things Reg had going for him—his meals cooked just the way he liked them, his clothes washed and ironed, a sexually willing wife—what more could he want? What was his problem?

Once Jean's opinions ran out, God's thoughts began to creep in. He reminded Jean that two months after their wedding, Reg's partners in his advertising firm misspent company assets, forcing them out of business and Reg out of an income. Jean became disabled shortly thereafter and lost her job as well, leaving them all but homeless. Then Reg's mother died, suddenly and unexpectedly. With little time or space to grieve, Reg had to find a place for his family to live, so they moved to Cornwall. But that didn't work out, and Reg was forced to move his family into his father's house in London.

Jean found herself speechless as these events rolled through her mind. She had been so full of words with the vicar. With God, not so much.

She later told the vicar, "As I sat there in that church, looking back into the past, it slowly dawned on me how all this must have affected Reg. His dreams had all been shattered in two short months—firm collapsed, mother dead, home gone—and he was back where he had started. He must have felt an utter failure. No wonder he seemed to turn against me and our son. He had to use us as a fuse, or he would have blown his mind."

It's painful for me to copy that last sentence. No, Reg *didn't* have to use his family as a fuse, but let's allow Jean to finish her story.

"I'd never before thought about any situation from another person's viewpoint. I'd never experienced such hurt as I now began to feel on Reg's behalf—my own hurts, hates, and frustrations seemed nothing in comparison. Tears ran down my cheeks for him and all the unspoken feelings which he'd obviously had no idea how to cope with."[1]

In prayer, Jean's angry accusations were transformed into tears of empathy. She was no longer a prosecuting attorney determined to prove her husband's guilt. Instead, she had become Reg's defense counselor.

This is the journey to which marriage calls each of us: to seek to understand and empathize, to strive to be a redemptive partner rather than a legal opponent. If we truly want to *love* God's sons and daughters, we have to seek to *understand* God's sons and daughters. *Have you ever asked God why your spouse is the way he or she is?* In the midst of your frustration, have you ever sought God's perspective for what has "bent" your spouse in his or her current direction?

I can never begin to repay God
for what He has done for me. But
I can love His daughter well.

We must be *for* our spouses as Romans 8:31 tells us God is *for* us. Remember, God was for us even in our sins (see Rom. 5:8). Do you realize that at the height of your rebellion against God, even then He was for you? That He was working out His plan for your salvation, softening your heart, calling you into His kingdom? In your most selfish state, God was beckoning you out of the darkness and into His wonderful light (1 Pet. 2:9).

That's how God treated us in our most wretched condition, and now He asks us to treat our spouses—His sons and daughters—with the same grace we have received.

Evil in a spouse cannot be excused, but it can be understood. Now, please don't take this the wrong way. I don't want any wife to try to "explain away" her husband's abusive behavior. (Please see the appendix, "God Hates Domestic Violence.") But marriage does call us to at least try to understand our spouses' struggles as God understands them—looking through the kindly, paternal eyes of a loving heavenly Father-in-Law instead of through angry, resentful eyes of hurt and judgment.

We can have empathy for others even while despising what they are doing. We can completely disagree with their *responses* even as we feel for their *pain*.

Try this: Set aside some time in the next few days. If you have to spill out your frustrations and accusations to clear your mind, have at it. God is big enough to handle it. But stay on your knees long enough for God to wait until you're finished, and then listen as He redirects your thoughts to see your spouse's life as He has seen it—the hurts, the struggles, the disappointments, the heartaches. This doesn't mean your spouse's actions will be exempt from consequences, but it does mean you will feel differently about those consequences and let them unfold with an entirely different, holy motivation.

May God so transform each of us that we learn to respond to evil with holy hearts.

Our Imperfect Kids Are Still Our Kids

One summer, just before my son left for his first year of college, I kiddingly told him that I could write down the first three arguments he'd have with his future wife. I knew him that well, and I knew exactly the areas where there was likely to be tension between him and a wife. At the time, he didn't even have a girlfriend. But when he did get one, their first disagreement was on that list.

And yet, though I know where he is likely to fail, though I am fully aware of the areas where my daughters are weakest and most likely to try *their* spouses' patience, it's almost scary to me how desperately I want my children to be loved. There are three people on this earth who could make me among the happiest of men simply by loving my children in an extraordinary way. I want my son to find a woman who will honor, respect, and support him even in the midst of his weaknesses and sins. I want both of my daughters to find spouses who will adore them, love them, and make them feel safe and secure, even though at times they can wake up with an attitude.

None of my kids is perfect, but they'll always be my kids, which is why I'll always love the people who love them.

It is no different with our heavenly Father-in-Law. When the rebellious tribes of Israel wept over their sin, God was eager to take His children back: "'Is Ephraim My dear son? Is he a delightful child? Indeed, as often as I have spoken against him, I certainly still remember him; therefore My heart yearns for him; I will surely have mercy on him" (Jer. 31:20 NASB).

God is fully aware of our spouses' limitations, and He is just as eager for us to be kind and generous with these faults as we are eager for our kids' future spouses to be kind to them when they stumble.

Women, if you dreamed of long, soul-filled discussions late into the night but six months after the wedding realized you married a man who wouldn't know an emotion if it bit him on the nose until he bled, try dealing with your frustration by understanding that you made a good God very happy by agreeing to love His son with all his limitations. Picture my earthly father-in-law crying at the rehearsal dinner, overcome with emotion because he believed his child would be secure in her husband's love, and you'll get a dim but compelling picture of how your heavenly Father rejoiced when your spouse made the decision to marry *you*. Your disappointment at perhaps not having the marriage you imagined is understandable, but worshipping God by loving your husband anyway is a precious choice that will be richly rewarded in eternity *and* will greatly impact your life on earth as well.

Men, if you married your wife not realizing that breast cancer or multiple sclerosis was in her future, and you're thinking, *I didn't sign up for this*, consider also how much joy you gave to your heavenly Father-in-Law when He could say on the day you were married, "I'm so pleased Julie (or Katherine or Danielle) is with a good man who will stay with her and care for her out of reverence for Me. I know what is in her future, and I will give this man what he needs to see it through. I just want him to take care of My cherished daughter."

One of the things I love about this perspective is that while "secular" love is based on things that constantly change—health, beauty, mutual enjoyment of each other, circumstance, and so on— my wife will *never* stop being God's daughter, so my main reason for loving her will never change. If she is an eighty-year-old arthritic Alzheimer's patient, she will be no less God's daughter than she is now. And I must never mistreat her, demean her, or do anything to dishonor her any more than I'd want my own daughter to be demeaned or cheated on.

What if I ran all my actions through this grid: "If a son-in-law treated one of my daughters the way I'm treating my wife, how would I feel?" Men, that's how what you're doing looks to God. Women, just switch the genders. Imagine one day hearing your daughter-in-law talking to her friends about your son with the same tone and words you use to describe your husband. How would that feel?

Things become so much clearer and evil becomes so much more transparent when we look at what we're doing through the eyes of a benevolent parent instead of an aggrieved spouse. I want to be a faithful son-in-law, one who makes God proud, who makes God smile, who makes God sigh with satisfaction when He watches how I care for and treat my wife, His daughter.

With such an attitude, marriage becomes a central part of our worship. Putting God before all else helps me to be meticulously loving toward my wife. Remember, we learn to love imperfect people by serving them out of reverence for a perfect God, who loved us in the midst of our own brokenness. "We love because he first loved us" (1 John 4:19).

Every believer owes God more than we could ever know. He not only created us but He redeemed us as well. He continues to forgive us. He teaches us. He encourages us. He protects us, often in ways we don't even know about. He provides us with a reason to live. His acceptance is the basis for our ability to face our shame.

When I owe someone so much, He can ask of me anything He wants. And one of the things He wants most particularly is for me to take care of His little girl.

Even if you spent ten years thinking about it, you'd still fall far short of understanding just how much God truly cares about your spouse. The Bible describes our believing spouses not just as children but also as "*dearly loved* children" (Eph. 5:1). A good bit of their comfort, happiness, and care has been placed in our hands. What are we going to do with that?

Let's not just seek to avoid grieving our Father-in-Law, however. Let's do our best to make God applaud our efforts.

Making God Clap

I once spoke at a high school football banquet. High school is that age when some males still look like boys and others look like men. Some carry themselves with the grace, authority, and confidence of a CEO; others look like a puppy afraid of its own tail, just waiting to be hit.

But when these boys' names were called to receive their awards, everyone found out where their parents were sitting. The clapping was a little too loud, the verbal comments a bit raucous. The family table always erupted.

Why? Because parents love to see their children recognized and honored.

If only we could see that God feels the same way. Oh, how He longs to honor the sons or daughters to whom we are married! How He delights in those who sing our spouses' praises!

If only we could see that it's not enough to refrain from despising our significant others. Christian marriage isn't simply about avoiding mockery or abuse. It's about *honoring* our spouses in the eyes of others, in the eyes of heaven, both publicly and privately.

Something I found particularly interesting at the banquet is that the clapping the MVP award winner received from his family was not any louder than the clapping for the meekest, most out-of-shape-looking kid who walked up to the stage with downcast eyes, almost missing the coach's handshake. That's because his parents didn't care whether he was the best, the bravest, the most improved, or the "iron man" of his squad. You know what they cared about? He was *theirs*. He belonged to them, and he was being honored. That's what made them clap and cheer when his name was called.

Your spouse may not be the MVP of Christian marriage. He or she may not win the bravery award or bring home the coaches' trophy. But your spouse *is* God's son or God's daughter. And God claps when He sees one of His kids honored.

Let's make God clap today. Let's honor His sons and daughters—beginning with the one you're married to.

Building a Lifelong Love

1. Write down at least ten things God has done for you for which you are forever grateful. You can praise Him for the way He has loved you, the very fact that you exist, His kindness in calling you to faith, and so on.

2. If you have kids—if you don't, imagine that you do— write down three things that you particularly hope your future sons- or daughters-in-law will be or do consistently in their marriages to your children. Are you being or doing these things in your marriage to God's son or daughter?

3. Why do you think your spouse is the way he or she is? Review your spouse's history, and determine what has been his or her greatest wound, relationally. What is his or her biggest disappointment? What insecurities do you think he or she might be trying to mask?

4. What is one way you can make God clap today by honoring His daughter or son?

2

Passion Sustained
through Purpose

How is it that two people so enthralled with each other that they decided to spend the rest of their lives together, who perhaps once shared an infatuation so intense they could scarcely stand to be apart, eventually grow so bored with each other that they can't bear to live in the same house?

How and why does a couple go from such high highs to such low lows?

Here's a clue: even the best of marriages is a miserable substitute for the ultimate reality of living for God. God created us to be people of purpose who live lives of eternal impact. When we settle for less, it's God's kindness and mercy that starts to stir something within us that says, *There must be more to life than this!* Because there is! And God doesn't want us to miss it.

The worst thing we can do when we feel the need for "something more" is to go looking for another romantic infatuation, which neuroscience tells us has a limited shelf life of about twelve to eighteen months. The way God designed our brains, it's physically impossible to keep infatuation alive with any intensity for very long. So don't obsess about "falling out of love" with your spouse.

Concern yourself instead with falling out of *purpose*, because purpose will sustain your love.

Romance alone is not enough to continually refresh our souls or keep love alive for a lifetime because no one human is capable of filling our every need. Our marriages must be focused on Someone greater. We need a *magnificent obsession*. We need to let the Lord of all creation capture our hearts, to fall more and more in love with Him. We need to make *Him* our desire, our very life and breath.

Marriages without a magnificent

obsession are racing toward

boredom. It's only a matter of time.

The magnificent obsession is based on Matthew 6:33 (ESV), "Seek first the kingdom of God." What does it mean to seek first the kingdom of God? Let me summarize it this way: seeking first the kingdom of God means that every day when my spouse and I wake up, God's agenda for us is more important than our comfort, our own happiness, our reputations, our enrichment, or our personal aims. We haven't just been *saved*; we've been *enlisted*. So our priorities must be radically different: "He died for all, so that those who live might live no longer for themselves, but for him who died and was raised for them" (2 Cor. 5:15 NRSV).

It's this magnificent obsession with God's work that makes marriages work. Let's be honest: none of us is so enthralling that we can keep another person enchanted for fifty-plus years. Five or six dates? No problem. Five or six years? That's a challenge. Five or six decades? Good luck with that. Every one of us has severe limitations that marriage seems to spotlight like nothing else. That is why human relationships that live for the relationship itself are unsustainable. So it would seem that notions of a "lifelong love" are little more than a romantic fantasy.

Unless ...

Unless we are "planted by streams of [spiritual] water" that keep our leaves from withering (Ps. 1:3). A magnificent obsession with God gives two people a reason to talk, a reason to get out of bed, a reason to stay together, and excitement that never ends. Marriage between two people with a shared love of Christ is a marriage that grows ever deeper over time. As God shapes our hearts to desire Him, He is also shaping our hearts to desire and enjoy each other. That's what God provides in a marriage centered on Him. So many marriage books talk about keeping the romance alive, which I understand to some extent. But too few talk about keeping purpose alive.

Long-term marital satisfaction is found first and foremost in worship and service, celebrating and working on behalf of God's kingdom instead of trying to create an earthly substitute. No matter how intense your emotional connection is, how thrilling and plea-surable your sexual life is, how successful your children are—these things alone cannot fill an otherwise empty soul for decades on end. You can have a good run with them, but there will be days when a creeping emptiness begins to haunt you. We were made to live in no less a drama than the spread of God's eternal reign. We *need* adventure. We *need* purpose. We *need* the adrenaline of stepping out of our comfort zones for a purpose higher than our own well-being. We *need* our lives to matter for eternity, not just for the moment. We *need* to find fulfillment in something greater than our bank accounts, our pleasure, or our reputations.

In the end, selfishness is a very boring life. Nothing, not even romance, can substitute for kingdom life because that's how God created us. Marriages without a magnificent obsession are racing toward boredom. It's only a matter of time.

In Christian circles, we do a disservice if we try to "fix" marriages without first teaching the necessity of fixing our lives on this magnificent obsession, seeking first the kingdom of God. I have no interest in offering people five steps toward becoming a little less miserable in their marriages as they live substandard, self-centered lives that aren't set on something greater. But I will tire myself out to help someone jump into the current of God's advancing kingdom. The best marriages are achieved by living for something else and letting that something else lift up the marriage.

But what if your spouse isn't a believer? You can still enjoy the presence of God in your marriage because His Word says, "The unbelieving husband has been sanctified through his wife, and the unbelieving wife has been sanctified through her believing husband" (1 Cor. 7:14). In this rather stunning statement, Paul boldly proclaims that there is enough of God in one believing spouse to provide everything a marriage needs to be sanctified.

God is that powerful. If your spouse is not a believer, he or she can help you learn how to love the lost. Meanwhile, seeking first the kingdom of God will make your happiness less dependent on having exactly the kind of spouse you always dreamed of and more dependent on obediently following the God you were created to serve.

Why Do You Want to Get Married?

When Kevin Miller asked his future wife, Karen, to marry him, her response was close to automatic. Later, Karen would admit that perhaps she should have thought a little more deeply about such a monumental life decision.

> When Kevin popped the question—"Will you marry me?"—no one asked us a bigger question: "Why do you want to get married?" At the time, the question would have bordered on blasphemy. After all, Kevin and I were in love—anyone could see that. We shared a commitment to Christ. Who needed better reasons than those?[1]

The Millers, authors of *More Than You and Me*, then experienced what many Christian couples experience just a few years into marriage: a certain restlessness seeping into the relationship. It's nothing stunning, nothing earthshaking. It's just a quiet question: "Isn't there more to life than this? I mean, we love each other and all, but now that we've found each other, is this really all there is?"

This is a life lived without a magnificent obsession. Some couples face the listlessness of self-absorption by thinking that maybe they married the wrong person. If they had married someone else, perhaps the marriage would be more fulfilling. But the Millers found it wasn't about anything lacking in either of them as people; rather it was about what they lacked as a couple in terms of a sense of *purpose*.

When their pastor asked them to take over the church youth group, a collection of out-of-control adolescents, Karen says,

> The group literally drove us to our knees. Before each event, we began to pray for the youth and for ourselves. The group also forced Kevin and me to talk more than we had since we dated. We needed

to plan together and present a united front to the kids. As we did, we found out a lot about each other.[2]

That's one of the things I love about joint ministry. You think you know all about a person. You dated for a few years, you've been married for another five, and it's easy to assume that you've got everything figured out, that there's nothing more to share, to discover, to talk about. Ministry of any significant kind raises a whole host of other issues. You see a side of yourself and each other that you never knew existed. Sometimes this can be inspiring, but other times it can be downright scary. The Millers confess that some of the challenges they faced and disagreements over what to do next felt like they might tear them apart as a couple. But the challenges forced them to talk and gave them a new reason to pray together, and a new intimacy was born. Purpose began to save their marriage.

> The biggest surprise was that through the process something good was happening to our marriage. We were working together at something. When we failed, at least it was *our* failure; and when we succeeded, it was *our* success. During most of each workday, we were miles apart. But when we led the youth group, we were arm-in-arm and heart-to-heart.

Kevin and Karen gained a new respect for each other as they saw each other's gifts put to use, and they stumbled onto a great discovery: "What a puzzle! That youth group ministry, which by all rights should have pulled our marriage apart, actually bonded it in a new level of intimacy. Without trying to work on our marriage at all, it had become richer and deeper."[3]

The Third Hunger

It was in this context that the Millers discovered what they called a "third hunger." The book of Genesis reveals three aspects of marriage:

1. Companionship (Gen. 2:18: "It is not good for the man to be alone. I will make a helper suitable for him.")
2. Children (Gen. 1:28 NASB: "Be fruitful and multiply.")
3. Contribution (Gen. 1:28 NASB: "Fill the earth, and subdue it; and rule.")

In one sense, we could call this third aspect of Genesis "joint fulfilling service," the Old Testament equivalent of "Seek first the kingdom of God."

If our mission from Christ is to seek His kingdom before all else, how can a successful, God-honoring marriage not be marked by mission? We're *not* told to seek first an intimate marriage, a happy life, obedient children, or anything else. Jesus tells us to seek first one thing, and one thing only: His kingdom and His righteousness (the two words define and build on each other, creating one common pursuit).

The Millers understood, as I have come to understand, that a life without this aim, or a marriage without this purpose, is going to lose a lot of its luster:

> We hunger for this today: cooperating together, meshing, working like a mountain climbing team,

ascending the peak of our dream, and then holding each other at the end of the day. God has planted this hunger deep within every married couple. It's more than a hunger for companionship. It's more than a hunger to create new life. It's a third hunger, a hunger to do something significant together. According to God's Word, we were joined to make a difference. We were married for a mission.[4]

A woman once wrote to *Marriage Partnership* magazine, "Over ten years of marriage, I have found that when my husband and I focus on our own needs, and whether they're being met, our marriage begins to self-destruct. But when we are ministering together, we experience, to the greatest extent we've known, that 'the two shall become one.'"[5]

Who Are You Married For?

Paul included an interesting little aside in his epistle to the Philippians. He warned them that so many "seek their own interests, not those of Jesus Christ" (2:21 ESV). If Paul were to examine your marriage, would he describe it as one that seeks your own interests or those of Jesus Christ?

I *love* the conclusion the Millers came to in the early nineties as they surveyed a pile of Christian marriage books at a bookstore: "It's like we're telling Christians to be single for the Lord but married for ourselves."[6] A sacred marriage calls us to be married for the Lord.

The First Prayer

Though every Christian marriage should aspire to seek God's kingdom as its primary mission, each couple will have a different expression of that mission. If you're raising kids, your first and longest mission might indeed take that form. But two people in a mission-minded marriage don't raise kids just for the sake of raising kids. Nor do they raise kids just to release two or three or four more selfish, consumer-minded narcissists into the world. A mission-minded marriage is focused on raising children who live in awe of God and who take their marching orders from Matthew 6:33, living out their *own* magnificent obsession.

Many Christian couples practice and promote adoption. Some of them have a difficult time talking about anything else and think every family should adopt. Our friend Annie, who has adopted five kids, once overheard Lisa and me just mention the *a* word (*adoption*) casually in a conversation with another couple. Annie practically ran across the room to say, "Oh, great! You *have* to do it. When can we meet? I can bring papers with me!" (That's a bit of an exaggeration, but not much.)

Some couples build businesses that employ families and serve the community in creative ways—they use their companies as tools to serve the kingdom. Some couples are particularly active in the local church, or in the arts community, or they reach out to sports-minded enthusiasts as coaches. The common denominator among these couples is that their mission is what keeps their marriage vibrant on many levels. Blessing others blesses *you*.

In so many ways, Jesus makes life simple and clear. As we seek to follow Jesus in our marriages, He even tells us how we should pray: "When you pray, say: 'Father, hallowed be your name. *Your kingdom come*'" (Luke 11:2 ESV). How many marital problems would be solved (or examined much differently) if our first prayer was always "Father, glorify Your name and bring Your kingdom rule to my heart, our marriage, and this house"? Seriously, if we made this our first concern, our primary prayer, the starting point for resolution, wouldn't we look at everything differently?

Notice Jesus said this should be our *first* prayer, but how many couples have never really prayed this prayer second, tenth, or last? How often do we jump over this primary concern—the glory of God and the spread of His kingdom—to address more trivial concerns? Our first prayer is far more likely to be "Lord, make him more pleasant!" or "Lord, make her appreciate me!" or "Lord, make him change!"

What if the next time you and your spouse reach a heated point of disagreement, you join hands and pray, beginning with the words "Father, glorify Your name in this situation. Bring Your kingdom rule into our hearts. Help us look at this through the lens of what brings the most glory to You." And what if, in the listening and talking that followed, you and your spouse kept this as your goal: *How do we, in this situation, yield to God's reign? What attitude, decision, and action will bring Him the most glory?*

Even better, what if married couples prayed this way before there was a conflict to resolve? What if we prayed to go on the offensive? "Lord, are we missing Your will, Your purpose? Have our eyes been blinded to something You really want to do through the two of us, working side by side in the day and holding each other at night?"

If you and your spouse are now empty nesters and have sensed a growing divide between you, why not ask yourselves, "Can we regather around a mission?* Can our hearts be knit back together by

---

* Some of you might well ask, "What if only one member of the couple cares about mission, or we care about radically different missions?" To the first part of that question, we do what we can with a sweet, uncondemning spirit, not passively punishing our spouses for refusing to join us but inviting them in by our firm and joyous resolve. To answer the second part of the question, there is no biblical law that the two of you must share the same mission and vision. But there *is* biblical teaching that you should encourage and support each other, so focus on that.

loving others whom God is calling us to love? And might that joint service renew our own love?"

Some of you are no doubt pushing back and saying, "But that's the problem! We're already too busy, and now you want us to do *more*?" Perhaps you are too busy, but are you busy with the right things? Are you busy with a trivial obsession or a magnificent one? How can God bless an aimless house? Where is He supposed to "push" it?

Purposeful Passion

How can you and your spouse discover *your* mission? Here's one exercise. Think forward to the end of your days and consider this question: If you knew you were about to see God face to face, what would you most want to lay at His feet? What do you think He uniquely created you to do? And are you doing anything about that right now?

Your mission might be a joint effort, as it is with a couple we know who has been working for years to get a film made. Or one of you might have a vision in which the other plays a supporting role—such as a husband I know who has been his wife's business administrator, book table coordinator, and support extraordinaire as God has used his wife to bless so many people. But it's something you are committed to *as a couple*.

Almost five hundred years ago, William Tyndale was burned at the stake solely for translating Scripture into English. During the tumultuous days of opposition that ultimately led to his imprisonment and death, Tyndale boldly told a clergyman, "If God spare my life, before very long I will cause a boy who drives the plough to know more of the Scriptures than you do." You might think a clergyman would rejoice at such a declaration, but back then making the Scriptures available in common language was considered controversial and even a capital offense.

Though Tyndale's life was cut short, the seed he nurtured took hold and his mission was accomplished. Easily accessible versions of Scripture soon covered the European continent and laid the groundwork for the English Reformation.

It all began with a mission. Tyndale could see it, taste it, and picture it. If the Scriptures were made available in his language, a common boy could know God's Word as well as any clergyman. It was a mission Tyndale literally laid down his life to achieve.

Here's a good date-night idea: Discuss how you and your spouse would finish Tyndale's statement, "If God spare my life ..." What's your *dot-dot-dot*? What would you most like to see happen? That's a good indicator of what your mission might be. A common mission is a powerful tool for shaping marital intimacy.

You may discover that the more you and your spouse are engaged in purposeful spiritual conflict, the less you will be sidetracked by petty marital conflict. Jesus promises, "Seek first his kingdom and his righteousness, and all these things will be given to you" (Matt. 6:33). Let's give Jesus the benefit of the doubt and try it out.

Building a Lifelong Love

1. Have you ever asked the question Karen Miller asked herself: "Why did we get married?" Why *do* you think you got married?

2. What has been your primary marital mission up till now? Do you have one?

3. Paul wrote to the Philippians that some seek their own interests instead of those of Jesus Christ. In your marriage, whose interests are you seeking most?

4. Set aside a date night to discuss possible "marital missions," both long-term and short-term. Pray together about how you and your spouse would finish the thought "If God spare our lives, then ..."

3

Making the Last Things
the First Thing Today

What if loving your spouse because he or she is God's son or daughter doesn't "work"? What if your spouse still doesn't change? I've seen too many marriages where one spouse is offering heroic, almost supernatural love while the other spouse simply takes this effort for granted, presuming on the other's patience and forbearance.

God offers us an eternal motivation that inspired awe in me when I first saw it leap off the pages of Scripture.

Do you know why the Pilgrims called themselves by that name? A pilgrim is simply one who journeys to a foreign land. But they didn't use this term merely because they were traveling from Europe to settle in America; their view of pilgrimage was much bigger than that. They called themselves pilgrims because, according to their leader, William Bradford, they recognized that this *world* was not their home. They were inspired by Hebrews 11:13–16, which speaks of "strangers and pilgrims on the earth" (KJV) who desire a better country, a heavenly country. They weren't pilgrims because they had left Europe; they were pilgrims because they were sojourning on earth, awaiting the heaven that is to come.

The vast majority of marriage books take a decidedly short-term view of life together. One man, who has written many books I have greatly enjoyed, even wrote about having "a new husband" *by the weekend.* I get this. We want to know how we can fix our marriages *today.* The notion that we could experience a significant difference in our marriages right away can be a compelling reason to shell out money for a book.

Even so, I have become convinced that having an eternal perspective is crucial if we are to make sense of marriage in the here and now. If I want to love my wife with an excelling and God-honoring love, if I want to plumb the depths of what marriage really means and understand the glory behind this earthly relationship, I have to remember that I am merely a pilgrim here on earth.

Well Done

The Pilgrims lived, as we should live, with this glorious truth in mind: "For we must all appear before the judgment seat of Christ, so that each of us may receive what is due us for the things done while in the body, whether good or bad" (2 Cor. 5:10).

What Paul is referring to here is called the "judgment seat of Christ," a day that every Christian will face at the dawn of eternity. This is not a judgment of whether we will spend eternity with God; that is safe and secure in the finished work of Jesus on the cross and refers to a different judgment altogether. The judgment seat of Christ is rather a proclamation of what we have done with God's grace and provision in our lives.

The phrase "whether good or bad" could just as well be translated "whether good or *worthless.*" (There's a different word Paul could have chosen if he had wanted to pinpoint "evil.") We will be asked: Did we respond to the powerful cleansing of God's mercy by sitting on our hands and soaking up His blessings while filling our days with worthless pursuits and selfish preoccupations? Or did we, like Paul, work with the urgency and understanding that we must give an account of our days to our Lord?

The judgment seat of Christ is not about getting *into* heaven as much as what is offered to us *within* heaven. Our eternity will be stamped by the judgment made on that day, and the judgment made on that day will be rendered according to how we live our days here on earth. This was a central theme in Paul's teaching—and thus God's revelation—to the early church:

> He will render to each one according to his works: to those who by patience in well-doing seek for glory and honor and immortality, he will give eternal life; but for those who are self-seeking and do not obey the truth, but obey unrighteousness, there will be wrath and fury…. For God shows no partiality. (Rom. 2:6–8, 11 ESV)

According to Paul, there is no shame in seeking glory and honor but only in seeking glory and honor *in the wrong time and from the wrong person.*

A famous Puritan captured the passion of so many classical Christian writers through the centuries when he wrote, "This life ought to be so spent by us, as to be only a journey or pilgrimage towards heaven."[1]

In the case of marriage, the magnificent obsession takes us from filling our marriages with renewed passion by worshipping a perfect God who considers our spouses His children, to being filled with hope because loving our spouses well can earn us heavenly rewards.

Most people want to know how to make their marriages more pleasant or more fulfilling right now, but Scripture urges us to set our sights much higher because how we live out our marriages here can affect us for all eternity.

Do we, as we are called to do, live this life preparing for the new heaven and the new earth (see Rev. 21:1)? Or do we insist in our relationships that God make everything right this week, this month, or at least this year? If we are kind in our marriages, we expect to eat the fruit of that kindness within minutes. Most of us have little sense of patient endurance, loving without earthly reward while waiting for God to set all things right in the end. We want "a new husband" this weekend! We want "a new wife" after one sermon! "We've put in the effort. Shouldn't our efforts be rewarded?"

Well, yes—but not necessarily on this earth.

How might it change the way we view marriage if we accept Scripture's truth that ultimate happiness and fulfillment won't be found on this earth? God is such a good Creator that earthly delights such as laughter, friendship, good meals, art, sex, and conversation can almost tempt us to think, *Life doesn't get any better than this*. But God says it does. Very much so!

It's not that I have a problem with or lack of interest in good meals, wonderful social times, pride in children, and the ecstasies of sexual intimacy. Thank God we can enjoy His many blessings with gratitude and even worship.

If, however, we start enjoying these things with an attitude of forgetfulness about where we're traveling to and what we're living for, we'll lack the power, the will, and the perspective to make eternally profitable choices when we don't experience immediate payoffs. (What rewards of intimate conversation await a spouse caring for a husband or wife in the advanced stages of Alzheimer's?) When you love your spouse but are spurned in return, when you give sacrificially and are not even thanked, when you stay committed and are "rewarded" with a spouse's apathy or even infidelity, does that mean God's words aren't true? Does that mean God isn't powerful enough to save?

Some of you have read an entire shelf of marriage books and now regularly fight bitterness because none of them have "worked." The magnificent obsession moves our evaluation of what "works" to an entirely different era. God has promised to set things right, and He will. But He reserves the right to do so on a calendar of His choosing, not ours—even if it means after our deaths. This can provide great endurance for those of you who are disappointed in this life, who feel as though you give and give and give and don't reap the response from your spouse that many popular marriage books promise.

If we are living for life in the new heaven and the new earth, the spiritual riches that await us will help us maintain proper spiritual priorities here and now:

- We will choose the path of holiness over the path of whatever brings us the most immediate pleasure.
- We will choose the path of obedience over the path of ease.
- We will choose the path of stewardship over the path of self-indulgence.
- We will choose the path of diligence over the path of lost focus.

We can thank God that He offers us many wonderful times on this earth but still not lose our eternal perspective. An Olympic athlete in training will go to the movies, read a book, stroll through a museum, and have dinner out with friends. But she will never forget she's in training, and she won't do anything that will undermine her training. Not if she's serious about winning a gold medal. She certainly won't tire herself out trying to win the Safeway 5K race in Paris, Texas, the day before she runs in the Olympic trials. She gives up focusing on the lesser so she can save her best efforts, and express her most earnest passion, for the greater.

Ask yourself: *In my marriage, how often do I get trapped into fighting over things that, in the end, don't really matter?*

One important caveat here: This is not to downplay the horror of domestic violence (see the appendix). When I talk about enduring disappointments, I do not mean to suggest you are called to tolerate abuse. Your *current* safety matters to God and is of great concern to Him.

Given Scripture's focus on the importance of heavenly rewards, if I want to love my wife with a biblical passion and biblical priorities even more than I want her to celebrate many happy birthdays, I will seek to help her have a supremely happy death day.

Happy Death Day

"Precious in the sight of the LORD is the death of His godly ones" (Ps. 116:15 NASB). When I first read that psalm I thought, *What kind of God looks forward to His kids dying?* The answer is, the kind of God who knows what heavenly treasures await them.

The Bible presents God almost as if He were an eager parent on Christmas Eve, excited to lavish His children with gifts the next morning. He's excited about our judgment day because He knows our sins are covered by the finished work of Christ, and now He can greet us with the many gifts He has been preparing for us.

Shockingly to some, Jesus doesn't talk of equality in heaven. Instead, He speaks of those who are greater or lesser in the kingdom (see Matt. 5:19) and of those who will receive greater rewards or lesser rewards (see Luke 19:11–27). In a similar, negative way, some in hell will be "beaten with many blows," while others will be "beaten with few blows" (Luke 12:47–48). As Jesus calls His disciples to a higher way of living, He freely uses reward terminology to motivate them: "Store up for yourselves treasures in heaven" (Matt. 6:20; see also 6:4, 6, 18).

The writer of Hebrews stresses that not accepting the reality of heavenly rewards has dire consequences for our faith because "anyone who comes to [God] must believe that he exists *and that he rewards those who earnestly seek him*" (Heb. 11:6). Paul backs this up in Ephesians 6:8: "The Lord will reward each one for whatever good they do."

That Conversation on That Day

Notice Paul says the Lord will reward us for "whatever good [we] *do*," not whatever good we *receive.** This understanding alone can radically change the way we face each day of marriage.

On that day when we stand before the judgment seat of Christ, He will have a conversation with each one of us. During that conversation, we will look at what happened to us—including within our marriages—from an entirely different perspective, one that is virtually opposite from how most of us view our marriages today. I won't be rewarded for how my wife loved me but for how I loved my wife, God's daughter.

Jesus won't ask me, "Gary, did Lisa know your love language and honor it? Did she understand that you need respect and respect you? Did she have sexual relations with you as often as you wanted? Did she know your needs and strive to meet them?"

---

* Paul is *not* denying that salvation is *entirely* based on what we receive. He's speaking of a different reality here—rewards, not salvation.

Instead, He will ask—and my eternity will be stamped by my answers—"Gary, did you know Lisa's love language, and were you generous with that knowledge? Did you understand her need for affection and acceptance and love, and lavish her with that? Did you make the bedroom a place of blessing and mutual service? Did you seek to help her become all that I created her to be, or did you treat her as a servant designed to fulfill your own needs and desires?"

If I am living for today, then a "good day" is when Lisa notices me, appreciates me, serves me, and makes my life more enjoyable. I lived for years in my marriage with that as my definition of a good day. But if I am living for eternity, a "good day" is when I notice Lisa, appreciate Lisa, serve Lisa, and make *her* life more enjoyable because *that's* what I will be rewarded for at the judgment seat of Christ.

Consider the radical words of Jesus in Luke 6:32–35, when He describes what it means to love, and notice the promise of rewards as motivation:

> If you love those who love you, what benefit is that to you? For even sinners love those who love them. And if you do good to those who do good to you, what benefit is that to you? For even sinners do the same. And if you lend to those from whom you expect to receive, what credit is that to you? Even sinners lend to sinners, to get back the same amount. But love your enemies, and do good, and lend, expecting nothing in return, *and your reward will be great*, and you will be sons of the Most High, for he is kind to the ungrateful and the evil. (ESV)

Our reward will be great, Jesus says, not when we love people who love us back but when we love "the ungrateful and the evil" as God does.

If you are married to the godliest, kindest, most giving and thoughtful spouse who ever lived, *that* will be your reward. There will be no extra credit given in the heavenlies for having enjoyed an easier marriage than most.

On the other hand, if your spouse takes you for granted, you may never be appreciated *on this earth*, but the day will come—Jesus promises it!—when you see your heavenly Father-in-Law face to face and He says to you, "You loved My son (or daughter) so well, even though I know he never understood how blessed he was to be married to you. Now, let Me show you how I spend all eternity rewarding those who loved one of My children on earth."

You see how believing in *that* day changes how we define what a good day is on *this* day? We will look for opportunities to love, serve, notice, encourage, and appreciate our spouses, instead of being obsessed with how well our spouses are loving, serving, noticing, encouraging, and appreciating us.

Embracing this truth will produce endurance and perspective in your life. Consider the words of the apostle Paul in 2 Corinthians 4:16–18:

> Therefore we do not lose heart. Though outwardly we are wasting away, yet inwardly we are being renewed day by day. For our light and momentary troubles are achieving for us an eternal glory that far outweighs them all. So we fix our eyes not on what is seen, but on what is unseen, since what is seen is temporary, but what is unseen is eternal.

Elsewhere, Paul even directly connects judgment rewards with marriage and family life. He tells wives to treat their husbands "as is fitting in the Lord," and husbands to love their wives and not be harsh with them (Col. 3:18–19). He goes on to say, "Whatever you do, work at it with all your heart, as working for the Lord … since you know that you will receive an inheritance from the Lord as a reward. It is the Lord Christ you are serving" (vv. 23–24).

Those of you who married godly spouses might be thinking, *Will I miss out? I have such a wonderful spouse who is relatively easy to live with. How will I receive any heavenly rewards?*

By no means is marriage the only pathway to eternal blessing. Far from it! Jesus was never married and will be celebrated above all. John the Baptist, the apostle Paul, and many others who never married will be celebrated for their faithfulness as singles.

Mutual Partnership

Happily married couples who will embrace the judgment seat of Christ in setting their agenda for today can take Hebrews 10:24 as their theme verse: "Let's consider how to encourage one another in love and good deeds" (NASB). Knowing that God rewards acts of love and good deeds, how can you and your spouse encourage each other, pray for each other, and stimulate each other to do good deeds?

Again, lest I be misunderstood, this is *not* about salvation. That is settled by the death and resurrection of Christ. But so many passages urge Christians to be rich in good deeds, so partners in good marriage will seek to inspire each other to store up these heavenly rewards.

What better gift could I give my wife than to help her do something for which she will be rewarded in heaven? What if I prayed for her, suggested something to her, supported her, and encouraged her so that she became more than she ever would have been as a single woman? Not only will she receive the blessing of obedience in this life, but I will also have literally set her up for multiple blessings in the next life. It's the gift that keeps on giving—forever!

So you see, living for *that day* is not some religious form of avoidance. It's not about checking out of this earth. It's about checking *in* to this life with a new intensity and focus, as God's redeeming work reveals itself through us and sets us up for eternal rewards.

The Last Day of Marriage

When Jesus said on the cross, "It is finished," He declared with glorious finality the completion of a passionate mission (John 19:30). In just three words, Jesus proclaimed that He had lived a supremely obedient, meaningful, and triumphant life.

There will come a time when each of us is also minutes from death's door. As married people, one of our promises to God was to love His son or daughter like he or she has never been loved by anyone else. We men pledged to be our wives' living martyrs (see Eph. 5:25–26). You women were even urged to undergo training to learn how to love your husbands (see Titus 2:4)—you were called to take your marriage so seriously that you sought out someone wiser and more mature to help you succeed. These are sobering passages leading us to much reflection, diligent practice, and unending prayer and counsel. And since we are married to people who "stumble in many ways" (James 3:2), these are not easy commitments to keep. There will be some seasons when it feels difficult, perhaps even impossible, to love like this.

But there is a finish line! There will be a day when the race is over, when our lives come to an earthly end. And our goal for that day comes from Jesus' own mouth: "It is finished."

This is definitely *not* to suggest that marriage means gritting our teeth and hanging in there until the personal trainer blows his whistle and tells us the plank session is over and we can finally relax. It's more like loving each other as best we can—even if that means loving someone who struggles with depression or being faithful to a sometimes-distracted spouse—until the present earthly limitations are stripped away and we can build on the love we have shared for fifty to seventy years. Though we won't be married in eternity, we will be able to know each other and be known even more deeply with even greater joy.

We will look for opportunities to love, serve, notice, encourage, and appreciate our spouses instead of being obsessed with how well our spouses are loving, serving, noticing, encouraging, and appreciating us.

That spouse who has momentarily forgotten who you are due to Alzheimer's will finally be able to say in eternity, "You were so, so kind to me!"

That spouse whose moral lapses tried your patience to the breaking point, now glorified, will likely extol your love by saying, "I can't believe you put up with me!"

That spouse who has been your best friend, with whom you shared many seasons of laughter and, relatively speaking, few tears, will smile and say, "It was a good life, wasn't it? And who would have known that it could get so much better, to this degree? I never thought I could love you more than I did then, but now you are even more lovable to me."

Think forward to the day when you will see your spouse's body laid to rest, or you yourself will be the one lying on your deathbed, waiting for your soul to pass from this life to the next. Will you be able to say with some satisfaction and finality, "It is finished"?

> "I loved her with passion, drawing on God's power every day, until the very end."
>
> "We not only survived our marriage, we thrived. Today is a day to celebrate what we accomplished in life together."
>
> "I spent so much time in our marriage trying to lead him closer to the Lord, and now he is finally there, face to face. While I will miss him terribly until we are reunited, I couldn't be happier for the journey we accomplished."

There is a day, friends, when this marriage stuff will come to an end, a day when God will look at how we have loved His sons or His daughters, and we will be judged accordingly. For some of you, that will lead to many eternal rewards. God is not stingy when it comes to rewarding those who faithfully serve His children. The magnificent obsession lifts our eyes from earthly expectations to eternal hope and rewards.

Building a Lifelong Love

1. How can looking forward to the judgment seat of Christ help keep you focused and persevering in loving your spouse?
2. How have you previously defined a "good day" in your marriage? How will you define a good day going forward?
3. How can you and your spouse fulfill the teaching in Hebrews and stimulate each other toward good works?
4. In the end, when you look back on your marriage, what do you want to be able to say about how well you have loved your spouse? What can you begin doing today to help make that happen?

The Glory of Spiritual Dependence

Do you ever wonder if you just don't have what it takes to keep loving your spouse like you want to? Sure, you have good days and bad days, but sometimes on the tough days you wonder, *Why does it have to be so* hard?

The good news of bringing the magnificent obsession into your marriage is that this is exactly where God wants you to be. Let me explain.

Of all the things Jesus did that showed His faith in the power and sufficiency of the Trinity, dying so young was among the most telling. Think about it: How much more could Jesus have done on this earth if He had given Himself another thirty years of active, incarnational ministry instead of just the three? It's stunning to consider. He could have performed many more healings and miracles so that the church would have numbered in the hundreds of thousands rather than the few hundred who believed at His death. He could have written dozens of books rather than relying on inspired earthly intermediaries like Matthew, John, Paul, and Peter. He could have established churches, putting leaders in place under His authority so that no one would question them. He could have given us a definitive model for proper church structure, leadership, and practice. Instead, the church has debated these issues for almost two thousand years.

Why *did* Jesus leave so soon? Why did He leave the church so seemingly unprepared? The answer is clear: *He didn't.*

Jesus had great confidence in the Holy Spirit. He told His disciples that this comforter and counselor would lead them to do even greater things than He had done, and so He could leave with full confidence that even in His physical absence, all that would need to be done would be done (see John 14:12, 16, 26).

How many of us live with this same confidence in the Holy Spirit? What if marriage was designed by God in part to move us in this direction? The Holy Spirit is an all-powerful force, able to lift us above selfishness, small-mindedness, and weak love to embrace the glorious strength of God loving through us. But since we tend to live outside the magnificent obsession, focused and dependent on ourselves alone, God may allow us to come to the end of our own strength in marriage so that we might finally learn to rely on His.

So much Christian teaching today is about developing *our* gifts, improving *our* talents, and reaching *our* potential, yet so much of Jesus' teaching and modeling is about surrendering to the work of the Holy Spirit. Let's allow marriage to teach us to trust the Spirit. After all, He's God. He has proven Himself. He won't go into retirement or even on vacation. He's not inexperienced or lacking in power or wisdom or understanding. We can trust Him.

If we truly want to transform our marriages, we must learn the glory of divine dependence.

God promises through Isaiah, "He gives strength to the weary, and to the one who lacks might He increases power" (Isa. 40:29 NASB). Within the context of the passage, this verse implies that we are either weary or will grow weary. The subsequent verse declares that even youth will faint and young men will fall down exhausted. This verse also implies there is a task given to us for which we lack enough power to complete on our own.

Don't pass over this thought because it's crucial: *Isaiah 40:29 tells us that God will call us to various tasks for which we lack enough power to complete on our own.*

The "secret" then to a truly sacred marriage is actually a person—God's promised Holy Spirit. Because God is such a relational God (meeting our need for salvation by sending His Son), it shouldn't surprise us that He meets our need for power by also sending Himself in the person of His Holy Spirit. Jesus said, "You will receive power when the Holy Spirit comes on you" (Acts 1:8).

This isn't a Pentecostal truth or even a charismatic truth. It is a Christian truth: we *all* need the empowering work of the Holy Spirit. "What we have received is not the spirit of the world, but the Spirit who is from God, so that we may understand what God has freely given us. This is what we speak, not in words taught us by human wisdom but in words taught by the Spirit" (1 Cor. 2:12–13).

Since marriage is one of the most profound acts of worship any two believers can ever share, it is impossible to be married in a sacred manner without the Holy Spirit being active in our lives, helping us understand what it means to love, giving us the power to love, convicting us when we fail to love, renewing our hearts when we grow weary in love, and pouring out hope when we grow discouraged in love. As Rob and Amy Rienow wrote, "If you think you have it in you to be a godly husband, either you don't know what God desires, or you have set the bar way too low."[1]

This isn't just theological speculation. There are enormous practical ramifications.

Who Are You Asking?

Many of you are frustrated in your marriages because you try to live as if the Trinity weren't part of the equation. You keep asking something of your spouse and rarely get it:

> "Listen to me more."
> "Talk to me more."
> "Help out around the house more."
> "Have sex with me more often."

But when was the last time you asked something of God's Holy Spirit?

> "Help me to love more."
> "Help me to listen more."
> "Renew my heart."
> "Give me strength."
> "Help me to forgive."

You'll experience far more success and satisfaction in your marriage if you start asking more of God and less of your spouse.

Jesus teaches us to pray for the Holy Spirit to be given us (see Luke 11:13). This Spirit, we know from elsewhere, enlightens us, empowers us, directs us, and renews us. According to Ephesians 5:18, we are to be continually "filled with the Spirit." In the Greek, Paul employs an unusual construction called a "present passive imperative," meaning he commands us to *let* something be done *to* us on an ongoing basis ("let yourselves be continually filled with the Spirit").

I don't fill up my gas tank on Monday and then curse the automaker when I need to fill it up again on Friday. There isn't a car in existence that can run indefinitely without refueling, and there isn't a marriage alive that can keep pressing into sacred intimacy without *daily* drawing on God's presence and power. This is one of the things I love about marriage, one area in which God shows His utter brilliance in designing it: our primary human relationship makes us dependent on our primary divine relationship every day.

This may be one of the truths I stupidly forget most often, particularly when my marriage seems to be going well. Lisa and I are enjoying each other, there's little conflict, and then I slide into self-dependence. Soon I'm no longer asking God for the wisdom or strength to love my wife because I don't feel I need it. Everything is going fine, right?

Until it isn't.

We won't get far—certainly not all the way to a *lifelong* love—without learning and relearning the secret of daily dependence on the Holy Spirit.

> "God, help me understand her."
>
> "God, search my heart for anything that displeases you."
>
> "Holy Spirit, give me the initiative to keep moving toward her, especially at those times when I'd rather walk away."

Here's what I've learned: the more I regularly depend on the Holy Spirit, even when I don't think I need to, the more problems can be avoided or at least minimized before they even arrive. Waiting until there's an issue too big to handle is like deciding to buy a fire extinguisher after the kitchen's on fire.

God has promised to answer our prayers in dramatic fashion: "I will pour out my Spirit" (Acts 2:18). Notice He didn't say, "I will sprinkle my Spirit, drop by drop." God said He would *pour* out His Spirit.

It is the way of God with His people that He will often let us continue to fail and flounder and be frustrated until we learn to depend on Him. That's the miracle of marriage—it forces us to depend on God. And all life is transformed when we live in dependence on Him. It sets us up for success in literally every endeavor. No longer shackled to our natural gifts and resources—though these too come from our Creator—we are emboldened and empowered by a supernatural Presence.

There isn't a marriage alive that can keep pressing into sacred intimacy without *daily* drawing on God's presence and power.

We can either keep trying to draw from an empty well, trying to transform our marriages by asking our spouses to meet our needs, or we can turn for provision to the God who promised to "pour out" His Spirit on all who seek Him for what they need.

Which do you think is the better use of your energy and effort? Compare how many times you have said to your spouse, "We need to talk," to the number of times you have knelt before your heavenly Father and said, "I need your help in my marriage."

Be wary of trying to "talk it out" with your spouse before you've "prayed it out" with your God.

The Lawyer Who Became a Nurse

My friend Rett gulped deeply when the doctor told him and his wife, Kristy, that Kristy needed an operation that would keep her in bed for several days and require special care for a few weeks after that.

Rett is a cognitive man, a brilliant lawyer, but he tends to live in his head with concepts and arguments and a quick wit. He makes a good living and can hire people to do what he doesn't want to do. He's not used to playing the role of a nurse, which is what he knew he would have to do for his wife.

On the way home from the doctor's office, Rett blurted out, "I don't know if I can do this!"

"What do you mean?" Kristy asked. "*I'm* the one getting the operation!"

"I mean, I don't know if I can be that low-maintenance. I'm high-maintenance. Tank [their dog] is high-maintenance. The only reason our marriage works is because you're low-maintenance and you hold everything together."

Marriage is a long-enough journey that eventually even the lower-maintenance spouse is going to be at least temporarily high-maintenance. While many might see this eventuality as a curse to bear, it's really a gift if the normally higher-maintenance spouse will view such a season as an opportunity to step up, switch seats, and become the primary caregiver.

In case you're wondering, Kristy gave Rett a glowing report for how he stepped up, although she admitted he was rather relieved when one of her relatives finally flew into town and took over.

Here's the key: marriage presented Rett with a situation he would never have chosen on his own. Rett didn't choose marriage to learn how to become a nurse; part of his attraction to Kristy was the fact that she was so low-maintenance. But that's what he had to do now that he was a husband. Marriage called him to step outside of himself, depend on Christ, and, in the process, become more like Christ.

Rett followed and appreciated Christ the teacher, but Jesus wasn't just a teacher. Christ touched lepers, healed a woman who had been bleeding for years, and regularly made time outside of His schedule to attend to the physical needs of those He loved. To put it in language Rett could now understand, Christ on earth wasn't just *cognitive*; He was also *caring*. For Rett to become like Christ, he had to grow in this same area. He had the cognitive down—you weren't going to trick him with false doctrine—but could he learn to care?

What is your marriage calling you to do right now, maybe even today, that you don't feel capable of doing on your own? Instead of saying, "This is just too hard," or "This just isn't my gifting," why not hold God to His word? Tell Him, "Lord, You promise to give strength to the weary, and I am bone-weary. You promise to give power to one who lacks it, and I feel powerless. You promise to give wisdom to the ignorant, and I am clueless about what to do in this situation."

Let's allow the difficulties of marriage to teach us the glory of dependence on God. Let's stop depending on our own wisdom and strength and tap into the glorious power and fierce love of His Spirit.

A Fierce Force in Marriage

We often hear compatibility described as the be-all and end-all of a happy, successful marriage. Admittedly, if God said to me, "Gary, I'm going to give you the easiest marriage and the easiest life anyone has ever known," I wouldn't be disappointed. But what if your marriage could testify to God's power and not just your compatibility as a couple?

When we are motivated by the magnificent obsession, we tend to set our sights higher. In 2 Corinthians 12:7–10, Paul speaks of being tormented by a "thorn" in his flesh. Three times Paul pleads with God to remove this thorn. Three times God replies, "My grace is sufficient for you, for my power is made perfect in weakness."

Paul finally reaches the point where he says: "I will boast all the more gladly about my weaknesses, so that Christ's power may rest on me. That is why, for Christ's sake, I delight in weaknesses, in insults, in hardships, in persecutions, in difficulties. For when I am weak, then I am strong."

What if, instead of telling everyone how good we have it at home, we honestly testified to God's grace that keeps us together?

> "We're really not compatible at all, but God has used our differences to build in us humility we wouldn't have otherwise."
>
> "We've never been comfortable financially, but that has kept us on our knees."
>
> "We got married young, and the fact is, we both want different things out of life. But God is giving us the grace and power every day to unite our hearts and keep us together."
>
> "Blending two families has been brutal at times. Neither of us believes we could have survived it without God giving us the strength day by day."

Is there a "thorn" in your marriage relationship that you have pleaded with God to take away? Is there something you wish He would heal but hasn't? *What if that's exactly where God wants you to glorify Him?*

It is in our weaknesses—as individuals and perhaps as couples—that Christ's power comes to rest on us. Often it is only when we come to the end of our own strength that we make way for God to begin. If God resolved every person's issue, every child's problem, and every spouse's annoyance with our first uttered prayer, we would be weaker saints. We'd be weaker couples. We wouldn't display the power of Christ. Or we'd display it to a much lesser degree.

Can you thank God for that child who keeps you on your knees? Can you recognize why God may choose to allow the possibility of another addictive lapse to keep both of you living in dependence? Can you understand that the Father may not remove some difficulties you hate because He wants you to rely on the supernatural power of Christ whom He loves?

I believe it will change our marriages and our walks with God if we stop expecting every problem to be fixed and instead expect every difficulty to help us learn Paul's secret of strength in weakness and dependence on God.

"My grace is sufficient for you, for my power is made perfect in weakness."

Building a Lifelong Love

1. What is the greatest challenge you face in your marriage right now? Would you say this challenge is teaching you to rely on God, or is it tempting you to resent God?

2. How might relying on the Holy Spirit change the way you approach a disagreement, confront your spouse, or deal with an ongoing family crisis? Talk about what this biblical teaching might look like practically in your home and how you walk it out.

3. Have you, like Rett, come across a challenge in marriage that calls you to do something you don't feel you're particularly good at? How can relying on the Holy Spirit help you meet this challenge?

4. Is there a challenge God might not be removing from your life because you could become stronger through it? Would you be okay if it never ended?

5

A Monk's Marriage

When the book of Psalms was written, kings determined who lived and who died, which towns were built and which were destroyed, who feasted and who starved. These rulers could claim your fields, your spouse, and your children at any time without cause. There was no appeal, no jury, no higher court that would hear your case and possibly stop the king from doing whatever he wanted to do.

All of this makes Psalm 146 (which has a lot to say about marriage by implication) an unusually radical call. The psalmist said straight-out, "Do not put your trust in princes, in human beings, who cannot save" (v. 3). This advice may not sound shocking to people living in a democracy, but when these words were written, every reader would have been sorely tempted to go to great lengths to curry favor with the prince because in many ways the prince *could* offer salvation—or at least seem to.

But the psalmist reminded the people that the king was merely a man who would die (v. 4), and when he died, everything he had, including their favor with him, would die too. And then where would they be? In contrast, the psalmist said, "Blessed is he whose help is the God of Jacob, whose hope is in the LORD" (v. 5 NASB).

Why put your trust in a God you cannot see or hear over a human ruler who can offer you riches or condemn you to devastating poverty? Well, the psalmist says, let's look at this from another perspective. God made all there is (v. 6); He provides justice for the oppressed, food for the hungry, freedom for prisoners, healing for the sick, and encouragement for the discouraged (vv. 7–8); He "thwarts the way of the wicked," and His reign, far from ending at death, will be "forever ... to all generations" (vv. 9–10 NASB).

You and I can't truly understand this psalm unless we recognize that it made perfect sense to the people of the day to trust in earthly kings and princes whom they *could* see rather than in a deity whom they could not. Psalm 146 was a radical call to realign one's trust and dependency.

Today, *many of us choose to trust in spouses we can see rather than God, whom we cannot.* If we're feeling lonely, we want to know, *Why aren't our spouses more relational?* If we're poor, *Why don't our spouses work harder or contribute more?* If we're sick, *Why aren't our spouses better caretakers?* If we're discouraged, *Why aren't our spouses more empathetic?* While it makes perfect sense to look to our spouses for answers, to put our trust in a mortal man or woman rather than the immortal God is to spurn the One who rules heaven and earth in favor of one whose body will, sooner or later, become part of the earth.

Of course we are to love our spouses, but that is very different from *depending* on our spouses. We are meant to put our trust in the God we can't see because He's far more reliable than a spouse we can see but whose power (and character) is so severely limited.

If you're tempted to say, "But my spouse *should* do x or y," consider this: What if your spouse had a severe stroke from which he or she never fully recovered? Would you expect anything of your spouse then? Wouldn't you then be forced to rely on God? That's what the psalmist was saying. To depend on a mortal man or woman is to place your trust in one whose strength and ability to love are limited and whose days will eventually cease. Sooner or later, you will have to do without your spouse, one way or another, so learn to trust in God now.

We need to be married people with a monk's heart.

Married Like a Monk

Fourteenth-century Augustinian monk Walter Hilton mimicked many classical writers when he urged believers to pursue the spirit of detachment, to the point where we "put no kind of trust in the possession of any worldly goods, or in the help or favor of any worldly friend, but principally and entirely in God. For if he does otherwise, he binds himself to the world, and therefore he cannot be free to think about God."[1]

This kind of detachment might seem a tad difficult in marriage, and theologically you might even (quite correctly, in one sense) consider it an attack on Christian community and fellowship. However, it does contain some helpful and profound advice for marriage.

Isn't it true that many marital arguments result from disappointment with our spouses? We want them to be something or do something that they aren't or they don't, and we feel sorry for ourselves. We really do want them to love us like God loves us. We expect them to just know when we've had a hard day; to know that we're lying when we say, "Don't worry, it's no big deal," and actually do something special for us; to know when we need them to be strong or soft, to yield or to hold firm, just because that's what we want them to do. If they truly loved us, they would know, right?

Don't you think or feel that way sometimes?

You do recognize that's an impossible burden for a human spouse, right?

But what if we sought a "monk's marriage"? What if we decided we would depend on God alone, expecting nothing from our spouses but depending on God for all our needs, including emotional and relational needs? Then, instead of resenting what our spouses don't do, we'd be overwhelmed (in a good way) by every little thing he or she does do. We would be filled with gratitude instead of resentment.

> We can make our marriages God-focused only if we obey His commandment to love instead of giving in to the lust to *be loved.*

In 2010, after fifteen years of self-employment, I was hired as writer-in-residence at Second Baptist Church in Houston, Texas. On my first day, I was blown away when a church staff member said, "We need to give you a new phone and a new laptop." As a self-employed person, nobody had ever purchased anything for me. Why was Second Baptist going to give me these things when they were already providing me a paycheck? For one thing, there were security reasons. They needed to set up my laptop and phone in such a way as to ensure sensitive church information wasn't compromised. Also, my platforms needed to be compatible with those of the rest of the church staff. Still, I kept thinking, *They're not only paying me, they're giving me free stuff!*

I could already imagine, though, that as time wore on, I might start thinking, *When do I get a new laptop? This one is getting kind of old. And my old phone battery now has to be charged three times a day!*

In that moment, I would move from gratitude to resentment because I'll have begun expecting what used to delight me.

Isn't that exactly what happens in marriage? When you're dating someone and he does something nice for you, you think, *How wonderful!* If you marry him and he doesn't maintain a certain threshold of gift-giving, you think, *This is all he got me? Seriously?*

That's why I want a monk's marriage. I want the benefits of being married to a godly woman while keeping a monk's attitude—expecting nothing, depending on God, and so being genuinely grateful for whatever my spouse chooses to bless me with.

I realize we can take this too far. God won't fertilize your yard when your spouse is watching the game. God won't meet your sexual needs. Sure, there are duties that seem reasonable and we want our spouses to meet, but let me put this in another context: Would you expect a spouse with a broken back to fertilize your yard? Would you expect a woman in an advanced state of Alzheimer's to meet your sexual needs? The time may come when your spouse simply can't meet those "legitimate" needs, and what will you do then?

Now let me ask, if it's *"can't* meet those needs" or *"won't* meet those needs," does it really matter, as far as our call to love our spouses is concerned? Aren't we allowing them to hold our contentment hostage in either case?

Pride and the Love of Praise

The *Philokalia* is a compendium of works written between the fourth and fifteenth centuries by authors of the Eastern Orthodox tradition. Originally written to instruct monks in prayer and the spiritual life, the *Philokalia* persistently—almost obsessively—warns against the love of praise and esteem by others, calling this desire one of the gravest spiritual ills and one of three poisonous passions through which all other sins flow. There's a lot of Bible to back these ideas. For example:

> [We did not] seek praise from mortals, whether from you or from others." (1 Thess. 2:6 NRSV)

> Am I now seeking the approval of man, or of God? Or am I trying to please man? If I were still trying to please man, I would not be a servant of Christ. (Gal. 1:10 ESV)

Even so, many of the pastoral calls I receive from married people concern a spouse who isn't getting what he or she wants from the other spouse. The monks may be on to something here—their warnings may be even truer in marriage. Isn't the lust for praise the spiritual disposition that ruins so much marital satisfaction?

> "Notice me!"
> "Appreciate me!"
> "Thank me!"
> "Don't take me for granted!"
> "He doesn't even see me anymore!"
> "I can't remember the last time she was affectionate toward me!"

We think of these sentiments as "rights" rather than temptations, so we read marriage books and go to marriage seminars in the hope that at last our spouses will "get it." In the *Philokalia*, these demands are presented as evidence of hearts subject to idolatry, not yet set on and content in God. They are proof that we are looking to the world to provide something that we find only in the divine relationship.

We need to accept that the love of praise is a sin, that the desire to be noticed and appreciated by others is just a fool's errand. (Can we ever feel appreciated enough?) If we will recognize that the need for praise is evidence of a heart focused on the wrong things, we can begin to turn our marriages around. We can make our marriages God-focused only if we obey His commandment to love instead of giving in to the lust to *be loved*.

From the perspective of the *Philokalia*, lust isn't just when a husband mentally undresses another woman; lust is also when the husband chews on resentment because it's been a while since his wife thanked him for working so hard. Lust isn't just when a wife sighs when the leading man of her day removes his shirt; lust is also when the wife demands that her husband consider her more beautiful than all other women. I'm talking about the lust of wanting—even demanding—to be praised, thanked, noticed.

Do we live to please humans, to be noticed by them and appreciated by them, or do we live to please God? Reread Galatians 1:10 and see how important this distinction is. We think the problem is our spouses' insensitivity, apathy, or cruelty. But time and again, both Scripture and the Christian classics point to our pride as the real enemy of marriage and Christlikeness.

Which is more likely to lead to true marital satisfaction—getting a fallen spouse to change his or her ways or changing your own focus so that you draw your affirmation from the God who will never disappoint, never turn you away?

Best of Both Worlds

Many monks and nuns have lived supremely happy lives without a romantic partner to affirm them, check in on them, buy them thoughtful presents, or ask about their day. Why? They looked to God for affirmation and meaning.

We married people can enjoy the best of both worlds with a change of attitude based on the magnificent obsession: looking to God as our primary affirmer and source of happiness while occasionally being surprised and grateful whenever our spouses add something to our lives. The difference is a marriage based on gratitude, not expectations.

I have found that the less I expect from my spouse in this regard, the more I appreciate her. This practice has increased my affections immeasurably, making me newly sensitive to every received kindness instead of bitterly resentful over every perceived withholding.

"Do not trust in princes, in mortal man, in whom there is no salvation."

Building a Lifelong Love

1. What does Psalm 146 teach us about the dangers of allowing a fallen human being—even a spouse—to have so much power over our sense of acceptance and our life satisfaction?

2. How can you distinguish between healthy desire and mutual dependence within your marriage and an unhealthy lust to be noticed and appreciated?

3. Why do you think we were so grateful for the little things our spouses did when they were still boyfriends and girlfriends, when we're now so ungrateful for the things they do as our spouses? How can you avoid taking your spouse for granted?

4. What can you begin doing to draw more affirmation from your God so that you're less demanding of your spouse?

A Marriage Worthy
of Our Calling

Once we understand that the magnificent obsession is, at least in part, a *call* to seek first the kingdom of God, we'll want to build marriages that are worthy of this high calling.

What does that mean? Consider this passage from Ephesians 4:1–3:

> [I] beg you to lead a life worthy of your calling, for you have been called by God. Always be humble and gentle. Be patient with each other, making allowance for each other's faults because of your love. Make every effort to keep yourselves united in the Spirit, binding yourselves together with peace. (NLT)

In this passage, Paul was addressing how sons and daughters of God ought to behave toward one another. What if we narrow the focus of the passage so that it specifically addresses a son of God and daughter of God who are joined in the most intimate of relationships? It might read something like this:

> I beg you to *build a marriage* worthy of your call-
> ing, for you have been called by God. Always be
> humble and gentle. Be patient with each other,
> making allowance for each other's faults because
> of your love. Make every effort to keep yourselves
> united in the Spirit, binding yourselves together
> with peace.

This notion of a marriage worthy of our calling recognizes that we have been enlisted in the most glorious work ever known: the advancement of God's kingdom, which we have been calling the "magnificent obsession." This gives not only a certain dignity to our marriages but also something for us to aim for. Happiness is a wonderful thing and an understandable goal, but a magnificent obsession is even bigger. Not at war with our happiness, just bigger. Wanting to build a marriage worthy of our calling motivates me to work on creating a certain kind of marriage dedicated to a very particular purpose.

So what does it look like to live a life or build a marriage worthy of our calling? According to Paul, we need to be humble and gentle. Let's pause for a moment to consider this. Do you remember how Jesus described Himself in Matthew 11:29? Keep in mind that Jesus almost never used virtues to describe Himself, preferring instead to use imagery such as the light of the world, the gate, the good shepherd. In the one instance where Jesus did use virtues, He said, "I am gentle and humble in heart."

So building a marriage worthy of our calling means creating a marriage in which the character of Jesus is displayed for all to see. More than seeking to build the kind of marriage *we* want, we should seek to build the kind of marriage that *serves our calling.* That means being gentle with our spouses because Jesus is gentle with His church. Without His example, we may never aspire to gentleness or humility in our marriages. We may prefer compatibility or security or even something as wonderful as laughter. There is nothing wrong with these things, but there *is* something seriously wrong in a relationship that lacks gentleness and humility. Yet not once have I ever received an email or office visit from a couple asking me, "How can we be more gentle and humble in our relationship?" Couples are so conscious of trying to achieve the kind of marriage they want but rarely give much thought to achieving the kind of marriage that's worthy of their calling.

God created your spouse, so consider it a joy to worship Him by celebrating this unique expression of His creative genius.

Another aspect of marriage that will make it worthy of our calling is not acting or speaking harshly with each other. We must not "lord it over" one another. We need to be servants, mutually caring for each other (Matt. 20:25–28). This is what best models our calling. When people see the way we treat each other, they should be reminded of Jesus.

"Always be humble and gentle." When Paul wrote these words to a Greek audience, he knew that the Greek culture despised humility, yet he extolled it for this reason: Jesus embodied humility, so we must proclaim Jesus to the world by being humble. Pride kills relationships and devastates marriages. Therefore, pride is unworthy of our calling to proclaim a Savior who "made himself nothing by taking the very nature of a servant" (Phil. 2:7).

Do you see the difference? Instead of trying to build the marriage *I* want, the magnificent obsession leads me to try to build the kind of marriage that reveals Jesus to the world.

Paul tells us we are also to be "patient with each other, making allowance for each other's faults because of your love." We've read James 3:2 ("We all stumble in many ways"), so we know our partners will stumble at times. But because of the love within us by God's Holy Spirit, we will make allowances for each other rather than judging each other. *We will show the world that Christian couples treat sin with grace.* "Making allowance" means being sensitive about each other's weaknesses and idiosyncrasies, knowing that the quirkiness of our natures sometimes needs to be accommodated. We do this with joy and a good spirit, choosing to encourage each other with uplifting words instead of tearing each other down. God created your spouse, so consider it a joy to worship Him by celebrating this unique expression of His creative genius.

It's important to note that, because of our calling, Paul also urges us to "make *every* effort" to keep ourselves united in the Spirit. This requires that we work diligently to be reconciled to each other, to quickly forgive and even more quickly ask for forgiveness, to resolve our differences, and even seek counseling if our relationship is seriously faltering. We don't give up on reconciliation—we make *every effort* to remain united.

John Stott called the attitudes expressed in Ephesians 4:1–3 the "five foundation stones" of Christian unity: humility, gentleness, patience, forbearance, and love.[1] These attitudes mark our marriages as worthy of our calling. (Of course, sometimes we may have to apply these unilaterally—that is, without our spouses' cooperation.)

So what does this mean for my marriage? I am dedicated to the preservation of my marriage's unity—not just for my happiness and my children's security but because of my calling in Christ. I will guard my marriage, feed it, work through issues, confront when necessary if something is threatening our unity, forgive with eagerness, and prevent bitterness by being gentle and patient so that I don't replay past episodes.

So many people seek to build a "happy" marriage. That's fine. God is into happiness. But I urge you to build a marriage that is "worthy of your calling."

Why not build a marriage that seeks to remind people of Jesus?

Do Your Duty

We will never understand Paul's instructions to husbands and wives unless we understand his primary message that our lives and marriages are not about pursuing happiness or fulfillment as much as they are about seeking first the kingdom of God. This is made abundantly clear where he specifically says that how we conduct our family is crucial "*so that no one will malign the word of God*" (Titus 2:5).

This sense of "doing our duty" as husbands and wives doesn't squeeze the romance or enjoyment out of marriage; on the contrary, it preserves it. It lifts us above our petty sinful natures and rests the success of our marriages on the perfection of Jesus rather than on our spouses' performances and imperfections. Marriages based on superficial commitments like a person's behavior are doomed to rise or fall with a spouse's mood and momentary decisions. But marriages based on the eternal relationship of Christ and the church will share the same delight and joy that the latter have for each other. In this sense, the call to "do your duty" isn't just a call to holiness; it's a call to *true* happiness.

Before moving on, let's review everything we've discussed so far:

- Our marriages will flourish and thrive when they are built on the framework of a magnificent obsession with the spread of Christ's kingdom.
- We can worship our way to happiness by recognizing that God is our heavenly Father-in-Law.
- Marriage teaches us to spiritually depend on God.
- Mutual mission preserves marital passion.
- Remembering the judgment day will impact how we live each day on earth.
- Spiritual detachment—not depending on our spouses to provide what only God ultimately offers—serves marital satisfaction and fosters marital gratitude.
- Focus on building a marriage worthy of your calling in Christ.

These principles comprise the heart of spiritual intimacy. You will recall that spiritual intimacy is the first leg of the stool providing sturdy support for a lifelong love. Next we'll begin discussing the second leg of the stool: relational intimacy.

Building a Lifelong Love

1. What has motivated you to want to make changes in your marriage—your own need for happiness or a desire to build a marriage worthy of your calling?
2. What can you do to better exhibit gentleness and humility toward your spouse?
3. To build a marriage that more accurately reveals Jesus to the world, the husband and wife need humility, gentleness, patience, forbearance, and love. Which of these (there may be more than one) do you and your spouse most need to work on?
4. Based on what you have learned thus far, how has your idea of your "duty" as a spouse changed?

Part 2

Growing Together

A More Intimate Union

"No man is ever called to be another. God has as many plans for men as he has men; and, therefore, he never requires them to measure their life exactly by way of any other life."[1]

With these words, nineteenth-century churchman Horace Bushnell said something profound of individuals that is just as true of married couples, so let me put this in the language of marriage: "No married couple is ever called to be another. God has as many plans for married couples as He has couples; and, therefore, He never requires them to measure their life by any other couple."

You comprise one-half of a unique couple. No other couple has your gifts, your weaknesses, your history, your dynamics, your children, your calling. There is great freedom in accepting our couple's identity as it is: we might be strong in this area, weak in that, vulnerable here, impenetrable there, excelling in this, often failing in that, but we are a unique couple called forth by God to fulfill our unique purpose in this world.

God has established your home and your marriage, *and that's the life He wants you to live.* Never look to other couples to measure your worth; look to God to fulfill your call. Don't compare yourself with other couples to measure your happiness; compare your obedience with God's design on your life to measure your faithfulness.

Lisa and I are not called to be Les and Leslie Parrott, who have two PhDs (Lisa and I have, between the two of us, none) and who write and speak jointly (Lisa likes to say, "Nobody asks plumbers' wives if they can fix a toilet, so why does everyone ask me if I will give a talk just because my husband does?").

We're just Gary and Lisa. That's all we're called to be. We have no other map to follow and no other marriage to live up to. No other couple should make us feel ashamed, humiliated, envious, or proud. We don't have to live up to them, and they don't have to live up to us.

Become comfortable with *your* story, *your* identity as a couple.

Relish it. Never compare it. Just be faithful to the unique vision God has given to the unique you (and that's a plural *you*). God doesn't need another couple just like one He has already made. He is so much more creative than that. Rather, He wants to release and bless the unique couple that is *you*.

This next section is all about the two of you continuing to grow together as a couple as part of your own unique journey. You could call it marital exercise or simply a roadmap to grow together. Building relational intimacy has to be intentional, thoughtful, and prayerful.

Supernatural Science

Science and the supernatural are sometimes touted as enemies or even exclusive realities. Talking about "supernatural science," then, seems like a contradiction in terms.

But I use "science" all the time in premarital counseling, finding that the session in which I take couples through their Prepare/Enrich test results is often the most helpful and revealing session of all. The test tells couples where they are likely to stumble and serves as a general measure of overall compatibility.

As a tool, it can be very revealing:

"Oh, that's why she responds that way."
"That makes so much sense. Now I understand why he does that."

It also warns couples which hot-button items might threaten their relationship and suggests various points in the relationship that need to be addressed.

Some of you who are already married might all but flunk the Prepare/Enrich test. (It's not set up to flunk anyone, but it certainly reveals levels of relational vulnerability.) You and your spouse might be entirely incompatible in a scientific sense. But plenty of couples have risen above natural limitations to achieve more relationally than testing says might be possible. That's because the same God who is Lord over science is also Lord over the supernatural. It's possible to have "supernatural science" because our Creator is King over both.

There's an inherent weakness in personality tests that is too often ignored: the assumption that we are flash-frozen people whose personality traits are set in stone. This is the lie behind basing a marriage on compatibility more than mission. When we surrender to the work of the Holy Spirit and the affirmation of God's love, we *can* change, as Paul testifies:

> Your faith is flourishing and your love for one another is growing. (2 Thess. 1:3 NLT)

> God is working in you, giving you the desire and the power to do what pleases him. (Phil. 2:13 NLT)

> We all, who with unveiled faces contemplate the Lord's glory, are being transformed into his image with ever-increasing glory, which comes from the Lord, who is the Spirit. (2 Cor. 3:18)

Just as powerful, supernaturally speaking, is the Christian promise described in the Bible as the "unity of the Spirit" (Eph. 4:3). Two people united in God, filled with the Spirit, and jointly purposed to seek first His kingdom (see Matt. 6:33) have a *supernatural* uniting presence in their relationship. It is more than enough to sustain them and to build a future on.

When God enters the equation—not as an add-on to the marriage but as the foundation, the uniting force, the third presence, the empowering agent—He can *transform* us far above our natural limitations. Remember Jeremiah 31:4? "I will build you again and you will be rebuilt" (NASB). A truly sacred marriage points to a reality beyond our human limitations.

Your tests don't have to define you. Your compatibility doesn't have to be a ceiling above which your relationship can never rise. Your past hurts don't have to constitute the first steps in a journey toward divorce court.

You may never have the easiest or happiest marriage, but you can still build one well worth celebrating. Just as important, you can build one that honors God, that provides a witness to the world, and that shelters your children.

Even if your relationship is "scientifically sound," adopting the vision of a magnificent obsession and choosing to pursue a more intimate union can still take your relationship to an entirely new level.

I want you to think about more than just the endgame, however. I want you to learn to surrender to the *process* of growing together. Building a more intimate union isn't easy—far from it! It's rewarding, but it takes more than a little effort to get there. The goal of this book isn't just to build marriages that stick it out with gritted teeth. It's not titled *A Lifelong Marriage* but *A Lifelong Love* for a reason. Even when we face seemingly insurmountable challenges, marriage can build within us the all-important attitude of a conqueror. And that's what we are called by God to do.

Called to Conquer

After several sessions spent discussing his marriage, Marcos finally looked at his counselor and said, "If all this is true, I feel like I've just run my car into a snowbank, it has a flat tire and is out of gas, I'm three miles from town, and my cell phone is dead."

The counselor laughed and said, "That's a creative way of putting it. It's not going to be easy. But getting the car fixed and back on the road is going to be a story you can tell for decades."

Marcos had to divide his marital challenge into steps. First, he needed to be honest with his wife about how her actions were hurting him. Second, he had to pursue a new level of honesty in their relationship and create a healthy distance that would allow him to do the right thing even if that disappointed his wife. Third, being able to risk disapproval from his wife meant he needed to double down on his time spent with God to receive God's affirmation, encouragement, and approval. This wouldn't be accomplished in a week, a month, or even a year. But the counselor helped Marcos understand and commit to his next best step.

Facing the reality of where your marriage stands may not be pleasant, but be assured that restoration is possible. Maintaining the right attitude is crucial.

Luo Wenyou enjoys restoring old cars. He told a reporter, "However tired or hungry you are, when you hear the engine start after months of hard work, it's unbeatable, the happiest moment in life."[1]

Notice the principle here: bringing something back to life becomes more gratifying *when it's particularly difficult to resurrect.* I suspect that if Mr. Wenyou needed to spend just a short hour tinkering around the garage to hear that motor turn over, he wouldn't call it "the happiest moment in life." More likely, he'd think of it as just another chore, like painting the fence.

Can we have this same attitude while repairing our marriages, recognizing that persevering in doing the difficult work until we see results can be enormously gratifying? Instead of seeing a spouse's addiction, bad attitude, broken past, or financial calamity only as dark tunnels that threaten to swallow us, can we also view them as challenges to face together, realizing that when victory is won, the sound of a marriage finally working again will fill us with tremendous satisfaction? Can you see how overcoming these challenges together could actually take your intimacy to another level?

The challenges we face may not be cataclysmic. Perhaps we just have to overcome the ordinary challenges of not becoming lazy in our love, gradually taking each other for granted, or letting our sexual intimacy fade into mere pleasantness. If we don't want these kinds of issues to grow into crises, can we see the challenge of restoring our relationship as an energizing opportunity?

Paul offers a shot of spiritual adrenaline in Romans 8:37: "In all these things we are more than conquerors through him who loved us" (ESV).

Dream together: "If we get through this, how do you think God might use us?"

Jeremy and Ashlyn found themselves stuck in a vicious cycle: Ashlyn was convinced that nothing would ever change in their marriage, so why bother trying? She wasn't willing to leave the relationship, but she also wasn't willing to live in it. That's a miserable place to be.

Such a defeatist attitude kills almost as many marriages as do affairs. If you are frustrated in any area of your marriage, will you choose to live by your past experience ("I've already tried, and it doesn't work"), or will you choose to live by the truth of God's Word ("we are more than conquerors through him who loved us")? Do you see yourself as more than a conqueror or as one of the conquered? With God, the choice is yours.

Ashlyn needed hope before she was willing to do the necessary work to address the issues in her marriage. She knew that she and Jeremy weren't capable of changing on their own because they had tried so many times before and failed. She finally began to question her pessimism when an older woman helped her to see that more was involved in their struggles than mere "relational" issues. Ashlyn had never considered there was a spiritual element at work. "You can't be more than a conqueror if you never even engage in the battle," her mentor told her.

Like Ashlyn, we're in the middle of a war whether we recognize it or not. Spiritual, social, and personal forces are moving to tear all Christian couples apart. Jesus' kingdom is hated by many, not least by Satan. Why, then, are we surprised when Satan and the forces of this world attack God's kingdom, beginning with His rule in our marriages? Why, indeed, are we surprised when our own sinful natures fight back against God's best for us, including intimate union with our spouses?

To embrace Jesus' call to "seek first His kingdom" is to choose to enter into battle. To not be engaged in the warfare—to pretend our relationship, mission, and integrity aren't under attack—is tantamount to having a picnic in the middle of a battlefield and then being surprised when a grenade explodes under our table.

Rather than frighten us, this knowledge should encourage us because, although we find ourselves in a battle, God offers us the opportunity to become conquerors. If you want to overcome the natural limitations of your marriage, you need to believe in the supernatural power of God to effect change.

The Battles Before Us

Romans 8:37 does much more than tell us we should expect resistance. It gloriously proclaims something even greater than victory—that we are "*more* than conquerors." We are called to do more than just survive; we are called to flourish in our marriages. Those of you merely trying to keep your marriages alive have set the bar far too low. A lifelong *love* is all about thriving in a ministry-minded marriage that impacts others. If you want to grow together beyond your natural limitations, consider adopting the following spiritual practices.

1. WIN THE BATTLE AGAINST YOUR OWN SIN

The first thing you must conquer is your own sin. As God told Cain, "[Sin] desires to have you, but you must rule over it" (Gen. 4:7). Marcos was aware of his wife's sin, but he was blind to his own sin (passivity). Ashlyn needed to confront her own negativity and doubt. If we do not conquer our polluted thirsts, we cannot hope to maintain the high level of marital intimacy God has designed us for. Sinful habits such as gossip, pride, impatience, malice, resentment, and lust wreak havoc on marital oneness. The conquering, in other words, must begin with us.

We'll never arrive at perfection before Christ's return, but we are urged to continually engage in the process of growth: "Let us purify ourselves from everything that contaminates body and spirit, perfecting holiness out of reverence for God" (2 Cor. 7:1).

2. REFUTE EVIL WITH TRUTH

Next, we must seek to conquer evil in our homes by assaulting the presence of others' sin with grace, loving confrontation, forgiveness, mercy, prayer, and a daily infusion of God's truth, which protects us from the lies that bombard us (see 2 Tim. 3:13–15). This last part is so important. We must conquer the lies that war against us, that blunt our love and lead us away from God's plan. This means—and there is no substitute here—daily immersion in Scripture. Remember, we are transformed by the renewing of our minds (see Rom. 12:1–2). Christianity is based on truth, which means, by definition, that a Christian marriage must be grounded in truth. A husband and wife can't maintain intimacy with each other if they're not also maintaining intimacy with Scripture.

Ashlyn's time in Scripture reminded her that her marriage isn't the most important part of who she is. She is God's daughter, called to seek first the kingdom of God. Her struggles with Jeremy are secondary. Reading Colossians 3:8–13 opened her eyes to what she needed to take off (anger, rage, malice, slander) and what she needed to put on (compassion, kindness, humility, gentleness, patience, and forgiveness).

She was helpless to change Jeremy, but surrendering to the work of the Spirit in her own heart was something she could see happen day by day. Scripture reminded Ashlyn that her happiness can never be dependent on the actions of another person, even if that person is her spouse.

The world is lying to us every day about what will make us happy. I lie to *myself* every day about what will make me happy. I need to hear from God daily what is truly true lest I pour all my energies into pursuing something that can never satisfy. The one place where I know I will never be lied to is the library of God's Word. No errors exist there. No tricks of the enemy will ever be hidden in its pages. There I can rest in the refreshing truth that gives life and wholeness.

3. FIGHT RELATIONAL DRIFT

In the midst of this supernatural warfare, don't forget to keep applying the "science." Sometimes the best defense is a good offense. This isn't about making one grand decision but, rather, dozens of daily decisions.

It's simple, really: if we stop doing the things that sustain marital intimacy, the relationship withers and dies. What's sad is that we often blame marital drift on our spouses instead of the relationship. We say, "I must have married the wrong person," instead of "We haven't nurtured the relationship, and now it's drying up."

Intimacy is something we can choose to build and even rebuild if it's been lost. If two people want to rekindle their love, by God's grace they can just by doing the things couples do. Intimacy isn't something you "have" or "don't have" as much as it is something you *choose*.

Marital intimacy is built via thoughtful, God-empowered perseverance and the commitment to keep doing small things that feed relational intimacy. Marcos realized that he didn't need to "fix" his wife before he started to do the things that once made them feel so close—like kayaking on the weekends or buying his wife's favorite flowers "just because." In other words, he didn't have to wait until *everything* was better before he started making things a *little* better.

If we want to begin growing back together as a couple, we must persistently communicate; there is no relationship without communication. We don't let bitterness grow. We keep caring enough to resolve our differences, and we go to God to forgive each other's weaknesses. We reserve time for each other. We make memories between the two of us, which requires the intentional pursuit of doing mutually enjoyable things together, without the kids. We remain the best of friends, and alarms go off if anyone else begins to feel closer or more desirable to us than our spouse. We keep praying for each other. We learn to laugh together, play together, work together, and cry together. If there's not a physical reason why sex stops or becomes less frequent, we find out why our intimacy is on the wane and address it.

Think of this spiritual "battle" as dozens of different "swings" of the sword:

> "Instead of playing solitaire on my phone, I'm going to text my spouse."
> "Instead of streaming a sitcom before bed tonight, I'm going to ask my wife to sit and talk for a bit."

Keep swinging the sword throughout the day, and at the end of the day you'll find that you are more than a conqueror.

4. CONQUER EVIL IN THE WORLD

The final step to becoming more than conquerors is to conquer evil in the world together. When we are masters over our sin, immersing ourselves each day in the truth, and guarding relational intimacy at home, we can go out and fight on behalf of other couples and their families. This is the missional aspect of God's plan for marriage that seals our own intimacy.

Let's not settle for less than the best. God doesn't describe us as conquerors. He calls us "more than conquerors."

Addicts, God wants more from you than to merely defeat your bad habits. He would have you conquer yourself so that you can help others achieve victory.

Couples on the verge of breaking up, God wants more of you than to merely hold on and stay together. He wants to do more than merely save your marriage. He would have you conquer at home and then become an advocate for other couples who are drowning in defeat, starving for joy, and thirsting for oneness.

Dream together: "If we get through this, how do you think God might use us?"

The journey to a more intimate union begins with understanding that giving in to business as usual inevitably means drifting apart. You need to see that there's a war going on—a war that pits loneliness, apathy, and isolation against our God-given call to intimacy, passion, and community—and our marriages are at stake.

Yes, there will be fierce resistance every step of the way.

Yes, it would feel so much easier to just disengage.

What will sustain us in battle? Not our own wisdom, and certainly not our own power or goodness. We are more than conquerors, Paul tells us, *through him who loved us.* When we truly understand, rest in, and relish the love that Christ pours out on us (see Eph. 3:17–18), we have hope whatever our circumstances. We know God has our backs, will lift us up, and cannot be defeated.

It is a trap to fall into defeated thinking:

> "My wife is a hopeless alcoholic."
> "My husband will never get away from his game console."
> "I can't make it another day in this marriage. I just can't."
> "We will never understand each other. We're hopelessly incompatible."

Scripture calls us to rise up and say, "This day, in His name, I conquer!"

This might sound hokey to some of you, but for others, it really could be a powerful start-the-day battle cry. We know that wars can be long, that battles often involve momentary setbacks. But if God is for us, and He is, we can greet each day as a new opportunity to conquer, to gain new ground, to faithfully advance His kingdom. "This day, in His name, I conquer! Yesterday, I might have had my teeth kicked in, but this day, I conquer!"

Neither Ashlyn's nor Marcos's marriage have been completely "healed" today. But here's the difference: Both now have hope. Their marriages are better than they were six months ago. The small progress they've made tells them that more progress is yet possible. And both would say unequivocally that not giving up on their marriages has been absolutely worth the effort. It's not just because the relationship is now a little more satisfying but because husband and wife have both become stronger people, more spiritually grounded, and more centered on God.

"I hated feeling like a victim of my circumstances," Ashlyn told her mentor. "Thank you for showing me that I don't have to be, that in fact, I can be more than a conqueror."

Will you take up this challenge to pursue an increasingly intimate marriage so that you can in turn bless other marriages with the comfort you yourself have received? God's work in this world is far from done. That's why we're here: to keep fighting these battles. That's why we are being filled with God's Spirit: to rise up and conquer in His name.

Remember the story of the Mennonites in Belize? It's not what you have; it's what you do with it. Are you ready to defeat rather than be defeated?

Building a Lifelong Love

1. On a scale of 1 to 10, with 1 being not compatible at all and 10 being perfectly compatible in every way, how would you rate you and your spouse? Why?
2. To lay the groundwork for improving your relational intimacy, which of these four do you need to focus on most: winning the battle against your own sin, refuting evil with truth, fighting relational drift, or fighting evil in the world?
3. Do you live with the awareness that spiritual warfare is happening in your marriage? How might this affect the way you and your partner relate to each other?
4. What do you think it means to be "more than conquerors" in a marriage? What can the two of you begin doing today to be more than conquerors in the future?

8

Pushing Past the Power Shifts

Have you ever watched a sporting event—a tennis match, a football game, or golf tournament—and marveled as the momentum swung wildly from one team or player to another? Something similar can happen in a marriage when relational power swings from one spouse to the other. I call these movements "power shifts."

By power, I'm referring to one spouse gaining the upper hand relationally. One partner feels less secure or more invested in the relationship than the other, which gives the more secure partner more "power" in the relationship. If you feel like you're more into the marriage than your spouse is, it will feel like your spouse has more power because he or she doesn't care as much as you do and therefore *seems* to feel more secure. This perception of power often shifts through the years.

Power can be good or bad depending on how we use it. Scripture tells us that Jesus knew that the Father "had put all things under his power" (John 13:3). Our Lord put that power to work by wrapping a towel around his waist and washing the disciples' feet. He then told His disciples that "you should do as I have done for you" (v. 15), giving a clear mandate that any power given to us is power to serve, not power to manipulate, coerce, or harm. If we can learn to navigate the temptations and promise of power in our marriages, we can learn to use it appropriately in other social and relational settings.

The net effect of power shifts in marriage is often loneliness— the opposite of intimacy. Instead of two people moving toward each other, it feels as though one spouse is running after the other, who won't wait up. Instead of the marriage flourishing as an intimate union, it becomes a desperate chase, and few things make someone feel lonelier than chasing after someone else.

Loneliness in marriage is especially painful. That's why we need to know the typical power shifts so that we can grow through them instead of having our intimacy buried in them. Power shifts, if not recognized or handled maturely, usually give birth to bitterness and resentment. Then, when the power shifts back to us, out of our bitterness we use it as a weapon and do even further damage to the relationship.

Here's the key: every power shift I'm going to mention also has the potential to *build* intimacy if it is properly navigated with empathy, prayer, conversation, worship, and service. I'll talk about where partners often go wrong, but that's only to help us choose to do what is right by comparison. We can emerge from each season closer and more intimate if we choose to.

For the sake of brevity, I'm going to gender stereotype a bit; please understand that the gender roles I'm discussing are often reversed. If I keep qualifying myself, saying "him or her" or "her or him" every time, we'll both get bored, so please take no offense.

"I Want You"

"It's going to be a short reception."

"Okay."

"No. I mean, *really* short."

Brent was thirty-one and a virgin when he got married. He couldn't wait to *not* be a virgin. So when his wife agreed to marry him at two o'clock on a Saturday, he fully expected to no longer be a virgin by, say, six that evening.

His wife laughed, appreciating his life of faithfulness, and ultimately agreed to leave the reception barely an hour after it had begun.

I've performed weddings for many such guys who are "champing at the bit." The sexual energy (assuming he's not already sleeping with his fiancée) tends to keep him laser-focused on his wife-to-be. And so he is solicitous, attentive, and kind in the weeks leading up to the wedding. It doesn't take long for the bride-to-be to realize she has a lot of power in the relationship. It's comforting and safe and fulfilling.

It's a bit surprising how quickly sexual intimacy can become routine, however. It's not long before the wife may begin to feel as though even her naked body can't compete with a video game, "thirty more minutes" to wrap up a project at work, or the final quarter of a game on TV.

What's happened?

Power has shifted back to the guy. The wife feels she is now more into the relationship than her husband is, and it hurts. It's scary. She has committed her life to this man, making herself vulnerable, but she did so under different circumstances. Her husband, once so thoughtful and attentive, now seems like a completely different person who is much less solicitous, much less into her. Who wants to face a lifetime of trying to compete for her husband's attention with all the crass things of this world?

Men, we can do a lot of damage to our spouses' esteem—and our marital intimacy—if we presented one front while dating and a different front after the wedding, moving from being so invested in our partners to appearing only somewhat interested, at best. The prior intensity of our affection and interest makes our current apathy all the more painful. If you've already fallen into this trap, an apology never hurts (even ten or more years after the fact). We must own up to our immature, premarital response having been led primarily by sexual chemistry. (It can be much more than this, of course, but remember, I'm stereotyping.) Sexual desire made us attentive, but our attention was a means, not an end. We didn't cherish our wives exclusively; we cherished what their bodies had to offer.

When the husband gets sloppy in this area, he is setting himself up to be the loser in the next power shift—baby infatuation.

A Little Affair

> The arrival of my son had completely altered my relationship with my husband. Though I certainly expected my marriage to change once we had children, I was not prepared for a complete loss of intimacy. We had been a tight-knit team, albeit a motley one, but now we were satellites in separate orbits, crossing paths only when it came to our child. My friends with kids assured me that the situation was natural and would right itself over time, after the shock of our new addition wore off. One friend, a mom of three, went beyond that: "You can't expect to feel the same way about your husband now. Your relationship needs to change so your son can be your focus. Our brains are wired so our kids can come first. It's an evolutionary thing."[1]

Well, the "evolutionary thing" didn't work so well for the mother-author in question. She and her husband eventually got a divorce, and how do you suppose that divorce served the kids whom she was counseled to focus on first? I don't mean to be uncharitable. I'm just pointing out that beliefs have consequences. As parents, we have to fight to *not* let the kids come first and possibly destroy the stability of our kids' home, even when they're babies.

Women often hate when their husbands make the charge that it feels like they're having "affairs" with their firstborn children. There is some neurological support for this behavior, however. When a mother is nursing her child, the chemical oxytocin is flooding her brain, causing feelings of warmth and affection, and she is bonding with her child in the most powerful of God-created ways. For some women, these feelings can be just as strong as those experienced in an infatuation.

In fact, a woman doesn't even have to nurse the baby to experience this neurologic effect. All she has to do is *smell* the baby. A German study found that the mere odor of a newborn baby activates the neurological reward circuit in women who are mothers. Two similar neurological events are the pleasure you get as you begin eating when you're really hungry and the rush a heroin addict feels when first injecting the drug. The same part of the brain fires up in all three instances.[2]

This explains why some wives, six or seven weeks after the child is born, respond to the husband's suggestion that they leave the baby with a sitter just to get away by saying something like, "Why would I leave *my baby* to spend time alone with *you*?" Hopefully, she doesn't actually use those words, but the horror on her face when the idea is floated tells her husband all he needs to know about where he now stands.

Perhaps she's felt slighted since the wedding. Before the wedding, her man was so into her, but soon after becoming a husband he pulled back. She tried and tried to regain his attention, to pull it back to premarital levels, and she failed. Now she has a baby, someone with whom she is experiencing that level of intimacy she has longed for all her life. This baby is so focused on her that he cries when someone else dares hold him. She's been so thirsty for appreciation and intimacy that it's somewhat understandable that she gives her attention to the child instead of her husband. (She thinks the baby will always be this focused on her because she is blissfully unaware of God's divine remedy for baby infatuation. It's called adolescence, but that's still a decade away.)

Meanwhile, the husband eventually realizes he's "lost" his wife. She speaks tenderly to the baby in a way that she hasn't spoken to him in months, if not years. If the baby cries, the husband ceases to exist. They could be in the middle of making love, but that doesn't matter—the baby comes first. The power has shifted back to the wife. And the wife can do a lot of harm to her marriage if, ruled by these strong maternal feelings, she succumbs to the trap of becoming a mom first and a wife second.

Of course, it's not just women who get caught in this snare. When the men do it, the couple is set up to experience what I call "baby bouncing."

Baby Bouncing

Francine ultimately grieved when her husband, Jacques, fell madly in love with their firstborn child, Eliane. That might sound odd. Wouldn't a mother love the fact that her husband so adored her daughter?

Well, we're human. Francine explained it this way:

> I had loved and admired Jacques since I was 18. Our meeting had been providential and had changed our lives completely. The arrival of our baby ...

seemed to complicate things. Jacques only had eyes
for her, she was his little angel. I was no longer the
only one he loved. I felt frustrated, as if something
had been taken away from me.[3]

Although Francine isn't proud of this, you can kind of see it,
can't you? This man she had loved all her adult life was now pouring
his affection out on someone he seemed to love more. Even though
that someone was her daughter, it still hurt. And when we hurt, we
sometimes do hurtful things.

In this case, Francine eventually compensated by pouring out
her love on second-born Suzanne, who arrived four years later.
Jacques didn't seem to love Suzanne as much as he did Eliane, so
Francine felt justified in compensating by loving Suzanne more than
Eliane. Now she had an ally in her war of hurt against Jacques. It
seemed they had achieved a balance of power—two against two.

Without knowing why, Francine found herself constantly criticizing Eliane, making her feel as if she could do no right while Suzanne
could do no wrong. The issue, of course, wasn't Eliane or Suzanne. The
issue was spurned love between husband and wife, and it was being
played out through their kids. That's baby bouncing—compensating
for the favored status of one child by favoring another. The children
had become pawns in a series of marital power shifts.

One fateful week, Jacques and Francine went on vacation and
took the leisure time to listen to God. By inviting Him to speak into
their lives, the couple sensed God pointing out the dark dynamics of
why Francine felt bitter toward Eliane and why she favored Suzanne.
Not only did the recognition and resulting confession restore Jacques
and Francine's love, but Francine took it a step further and apologized
to Eliane, who said, "At last you've admitted it. You *did* love Suzanne

more than me. I knew it!" Eliane gave her a big hug, and deep healing began. This might seem like an awkward conversation—a parent admitting that she loved one child more than the other—but Eliane already knew what was happening whether Francine admitted it or not. Best to confess it, explain it, and use it as a pathway to grow and allow God's redeeming work to take place.

When a marriage gets sick, the family gets sick. To stop building your marriage for the sake of your children is like leaving them out in the rain while you cook their dinner. Don't bounce marital dysfunction from child to child. Don't let the dynamics of your marriage cause you to enlist your children in a covert war against your spouse. (It's not just divorced spouses who pit their children against each other.) If you feel neglected, tell each other. If you believe you've lost your spouse's heart, don't ever think you can compensate by trying to gain control of your child's heart. Our children aren't pawns; they're not to be used to soothe the aches in our marriages. They're to be nurtured, trained, and launched into their own life of love.

Talk to each other. Listen to God. Seek counsel. Resolve together that the child-rearing years will create memories, partnership, and shared purpose instead of bitterness, resentment, and alienation.

Checking Out

The next power shift often occurs when the husband realizes he has lost his wife to the kids (or her career, or her aging parents who need extra care, or even, at times, the family pet). Once this happens, he is likely to try meeting his ego needs through another avenue. One thing I've learned about men: if we don't think we can win, we usually won't even compete; we just turn our focus elsewhere. This is clearly an immature response, but if we can't find respect at home, we'll search for it outside the home. It might be at work, on a video game, at the golf course, or in a deer blind. But we'll stray however far we must in order to get some semblance of respect, somewhere.

This becomes a relational cancer when the other spouse responds in kind: *Okay, it's clear he has checked out. That reinforces my decision to focus on the kids, because he's not. He just sits there playing his video games. Someone has to be the adult!* "Checking out" is usually cyclical—each partner's actions reinforce the other's, pushing the couple further and further apart.

Resentment, like some forms of cancer, is patient. It may exist in the relational bloodstream for a decade or more before showing any symptoms. The marriage grows colder and colder as the relationship gets sicker and sicker, but it's a slow descent, so both partners gradually get used to being strangers who share the same bed.

This is a prime season for affairs, a lapse into addictions, or any other unhealthy coping mechanism. Lonely Christians do things they never could have imagined doing when they weren't lonely. And lonely Christians might even bring up the *d* word (divorce) when the kids leave home and there isn't anything holding the two of them together anymore.

One sign of checking out is that your social circles are becoming distinct and separate. Social science has revealed that many cases of divorce are caused not by an affair or abuse but rather by the slow, gradual loss of a shared social circle. As both partners find new social circles (whether at work, online, or at parent-teacher clubs), their shared social circle as a couple begins to split into two separate circles. This makes divorce easier and more fathomable to conceive because each partner already belongs somewhere else and feels he or she has less of a home to lose.

If you want to fireproof your marriage, ensure that you do the opposite of "checking out," and instead do everything in your power to "check in" to your partner's social circle. If someone else is important to your spouse, he or she needs to become important to you. Modern work schedules and online communities make it inevitable that spouses will build relationships outside of each other, but there should be no *significant* relationship that the other spouse isn't aware of and at least a part of (at minimum, by talking about it).

Here's a fun idea: At the end of every week, hand your phones to each other and look at who each of you got the most calls from. Talk about those relationships, pray about them, and become a part of them.

"Checking out" is the beginning of the end; "checking in" is the journey toward intimacy and joy.

Empty House, Empty Hearts

"This is the way to watch baseball!"

Graham (my son, who at the time was in college) and I were in sports heaven, sitting in the Diamond Club at a Houston Astros game, spitting distance (literally) from the catcher. My friend Skip, who provided the tickets, just smiled.

Skip is about fifteen years older than me, and I've found him to be a helpful source with whom to discuss common family issues that are new to me. My youngest daughter, Kelsey, was just weeks away from her freshman year in college, so I asked Skip what I could expect in my marriage now that Lisa and I were about to become empty nesters. Lisa had been enormously involved in our kids' lives. She didn't want or have a career outside the home, and now life was about to change in a drastic way.

"She's going to need more affirmation than you can imagine," Skip told me. Graham's jaw dropped as he listened, and we just looked at each other. We had both found that as much as we had tried to encourage Lisa lately, it wasn't enough. Now Skip was explaining why.

"Everything she used to get her esteem from is now gone, in a sense, and she's got to find a new life. That's scary. You're going to have to be more attentive than ever and keep building her up."

This isn't true just for wives becoming empty nesters but also for wives or husbands who are entering retirement. When something has defined you for most of your adult life, and that something has been taken away, doesn't it make sense that the marriage will be subject to some new stress? This is an invitation to step up marital intimacy, to become more engaged as a couple, to see change as an opportunity instead of a burden.

Most life events are like that: they can be opportunities to make deposits in our marriages by investing in our spouses' emotional well-being just when they need it most, or they become failed tests that lead to our spouses' withdrawal if we stay silent and pretend that nothing has changed. We need to see that doing the latter could be considered an act of cruelty. If my wife is swimming in a lake, laughing and bobbing up and down, I can just watch her from afar and smile. But if she suddenly tires and begins screaming and struggling to stay afloat and I simply watch her from afar and smile, that's unspeakably cruel.

The challenge is that emotional needs are rarely so obvious as someone drowning in a lake. Maybe our spouses are ashamed to admit their needs. Maybe they're afraid that if they raise the issue it will scare us off or that we will refuse to step up. Sometimes pushing past the power shifts is about unilaterally stepping up when our spouses need us to, without being asked, even if it means we have to study them to figure out what they truly need.

If your husband or wife retires and suddenly starts hanging around you more, you can respond in one of two ways: You can ask, "Where were you the last thirty years?" Or you can suggest, "We've kind of become strangers, haven't we? Well, let's see how we can regrow this relationship." The window is rather small, a few months at best. You're going to set a new pattern sooner rather than later. You'll either learn to stay apart even though your schedules don't demand it, or you'll learn to become a more intimate couple.

There's one more power shift I need to mention, although I wish I didn't have to. It is one that men, in particular, often don't handle very well.

Devoted to the End

It's heartbreaking to hear of women who were diagnosed with multiple sclerosis, cancer, or Parkinson's and whose husbands decided to take the medical diagnosis as an "escape clause" and find a woman who wasn't "broken." Did you know that seven out of ten men, upon hearing of their wife's cataclysmic medical diagnosis, leave the marriage?

I'm always shocked by two things when I hear these stories of abandonment: the stoicism and strength of the women telling me their stories, and the unashamedly selfish, cruel response of the men. (There are no doubt many men who have been on the other side in this situation, so please, don't feel the need to email me in protest. I have stated that I'm dealing in stereotypes, and I'm giving you your due right here.)

One man who challenges me to this day with his entirely different response is Dr. Robertson McQuilkin, past president of Columbia Bible College and Seminary (now Columbia International University). There was a time when Dr. McQuilkin and his wife, Muriel, were a "power couple" in Christian circles. Both were successful authors who often headlined conferences. That all changed when a doctor at Duke University diagnosed Muriel with early-onset Alzheimer's.

Because the McQuilkins were a popular couple, Robertson received every imaginable kind of advice as to what would cure his wife, until he finally told everyone to please stop with the suggestions. In his words, "We would trust the Lord to work a miracle in Muriel if he so desired or work a miracle in me if he didn't."[4]

This is such a stellar statement from a husband! Robertson had gone to God and asked of Him, "Lord, I pray You will do a physical miracle in my wife, but if You choose not to, then work a spiritual miracle in me so that I can love her well until the end." And that's just what Robertson did.

Muriel loved art, so Robertson took her to the Tate Galleries in London, where some of Muriel's favorite works were kept. Unfortunately, the disease had advanced to such a state that Muriel was already having good days and bad days, and this was not a good day. Robertson recounted, "A great sadness swept over me as I watched her rush through the gallery with never a glance at the masterworks she had loved so long." He grieved that, in one sense, part of his wife was already gone.

On the flight to London, Robertson had faced the embarrassing necessity of following his wife into the airplane's cubicle toilet. He saw the smirks around him, and he knew what some were thinking: *Aren't you a little old to be joining the mile-high club?* Yet Robertson followed her anyway because "I knew what they didn't; if she ever got the door shut—unlikely as that might be—she never could have gotten it open again."

At the airport on their way home, while waiting for their flight to leave, Muriel got restless. Robertson had learned that in such circumstances it was best to let her roam, so he trailed behind her, carrying their bags. He sat when Muriel wanted to sit and got up and followed her when she wanted to walk. Sometimes he practically had to jog, still toting those bags, trying to keep up.

Muriel eventually sat down across from a businesswoman working diligently on her laptop. The woman's dress and demeanor exuded power, influence, and success. Muriel continued with her ADD-like fidgeting, but she always returned to this same seat across from the businesswoman. Every time, Robertson followed Muriel to make sure she was okay. Finally, after they had returned from yet another short jaunt to the same seat, the businesswoman quietly spoke. No one else was around, so Robertson assumed she was talking to him.

"Pardon?" he asked.

"Oh," she said, slightly embarrassed, "I was just asking myself, 'Will I ever find a man to love me like you so obviously love her?'"

Men, think about this: a successful businesswoman who had achieved what so many desire—affluence, power, purpose, position, influence—was envious of an Alzheimer's patient, wondering if a man would ever love her as Robertson loved Muriel. It's a stunning admission of our passionate yearning to be loved, even when everything else in life seems to be going so well. I'm not saying this woman would have traded places with Muriel, only that there was a part of her that wondered what such love and devotion felt like, believing that she had missed out because she had never experienced it.

If we want a *lifelong* love, then it can't be about how a marriage can fulfill our needs but, rather, how we can fulfill our spouses' needs.

For her part, Muriel kept on loving Robertson as well, as best she could. That's what eventually led to his resignation. During the latter days of Robertson's college presidency, Muriel would chase after him, sometimes as many as ten times a day, speed walking on her way to his office. Sometimes she lost her way but kept walking, desperate to find the one person with whom she felt at home. One night, as Robertson helped Muriel undress, he recoiled at the sight of her bloody feet. Earlier in the day, she had so panicked to get out of the house to find him that she had neglected to put on shoes and had ripped much of the skin off the bottom of her feet.

That was it for Robertson. He decided to lay aside the power and prestige of his position, to give up the intellectual stimulation of the college environment to which he had dedicated his life, and stay home with his wife. In his farewell address, he explained that the choice, in the end, wasn't all that hard: "The decision to come to Columbia was the most difficult I have had to make; the decision to leave 22 years later, though painful, was one of the easiest.… The decision was made, in a way, 42 years ago when I promised to care for Muriel 'in sickness and in health … till death do us part.'"

As a stay-at-home husband, Robertson had time to read things he wouldn't have read before, such as a national advice columnist. He was puzzled at how often people wrote in, wanting to leave their marriage because the relationship wasn't meeting their "needs." The columnist's answers were fairly predictable as she laid out common-sense reasons to end a marriage. Robertson thought, *There is an eerie irrelevance to every one of those criteria for me.* Which one of his needs could Muriel meet now?

Instead of lecturing on the book of Acts, Robertson now found himself cleaning up his wife and her frequent bathroom accidents. On one occasion, he was listening to a popular radio preacher while doing so, and the preacher's dulcet voice challenged, "Men! Are you at home? *Really* at home?"

With feces on his hands, Robertson found himself smiling. "Yeah, Chuck, I'm really at home," he said. "Trust me. I'm *really* at home."

Robertson's doctor was deeply moved by the care this former seminary president was giving to his wife, and he told him how seven out of ten men leave their marriages when their wives receive catastrophic medical diagnoses. Robertson was stunned. "Just when they're needed most," he would later write. "I thought to myself, *How could they do such a thing? Maybe they're having a love affair. With themselves.*"

Robertson believes this difficult season actually amplified his and Muriel's love:

> I made a wonderful discovery. As Muriel became ever more dependent on me, our love seeped to deeper, unknown crevices of the heart.... My imprisonment turned out to be a delightful liberation to love more fully than I had ever known. We found the chains of confining circumstance to be, not instruments of torture, but bonds to hold us closer. But there was even greater liberation. It has to do with God's love. No one ever needed me like Muriel, and no one ever responded to my efforts so totally as she. It's the nearest thing I've experienced on a human plane to what my relationship with God was designed to be: God's unfailing love poured out in constant care of helpless me. Surely he planned that relationship to draw from me the

kind of love and gratitude Muriel had for her man. Her insatiable—even desperate—longing to be with me, her quiet confidence in my ability and desire to care for her, a mirror reflection of what my love for God should be. That was the first discovery—the power of love to liberate in the very bondage imposed by unwanted circumstances. People don't always understand that.

Robertson teaches us that if we want a *lifelong* love, then it can't be about how a marriage can fulfill our needs but, rather, how we can fulfill our spouses' needs. In an end-of-life power shift, God is glorified when we move toward our spouses even as our spouses become unable to move toward us. After all, that's what God did for us by sending His Son to save us when we were yet sinners.

"I Do and I Will"

The catalyst might be the death of infatuation. The slowing down of sexual chemistry. The birth of a child. The busyness of raising children. The quiet of the empty nest. A sudden change in midlife. The medical diagnosis of an aging body. Whatever it is, we can choose to approach this new season as an avenue toward greater understanding, empathy, and intimacy, or we can let it become a highway toward separation.

As couples, we can (and should) anticipate changing seasons in our marriages. The default action of most relationships will be to drift away from each other while we attend to the crisis at hand. We have to remember that we made a prior commitment never to leave our spouses behind when we're running toward something else.

Look at your relationship. Talk about it with your spouse. Is he or she suffering because of a recent power shift? Is your spouse running after you but can't catch you? Has there been a different power shift I haven't mentioned? How can you grow back together once you've begun drifting apart? How can you anticipate and prepare for the next shift in power?

Holding on to intimacy in marriage requires vigilance. Just waking up and going about our days, without giving the relationship a second thought, usually causes us to slowly drift apart. Marriage is not like a tree that grows on its own after it's been planted; we must have the mind-set of architects and builders, planning and constructing our marriages stone by stone, brick by brick. Marriage is not like the natural, seemingly accidental beauty of the Grand Canyon; it's far more like the completion of a great cathedral that has slowly taken shape over decades of dedicated effort. When couples say "I do" on their wedding day, I wish they'd add "and I will, *every day of our lives*." The catchphrase for an intimate marriage really could be "I do and I will."

Modern life dictates that we may not be able to connect conversationally as often as we would like as a couple. We may have to endure short separations to care for our parents and children. We may not be able to enjoy sex with the frequency we once did. But when we allow a temporary setback to become a never-ending string of such events, our marriages will grow dimmer by the day.

Do you want an increasingly intimate union with your spouse? Then you must work to stay close. Be eager to get back together when life events force you apart. Choose to remind yourselves of those blessed words spoken on your wedding day, "I do," and then add the phrase "and I will."

Building a Lifelong Love

1. Is there a "power imbalance" going on in your marriage right now? Do you feel like you are chasing after your spouse or your spouse is chasing after you? How do you think God wants you to respond to that imbalance at this moment?

2. What can you do to turn any challenge in your marriage from a crisis that's pulling the two of you apart to an opportunity that's helping you grow together?

3. Do you need to ask forgiveness for any apathy during a previous power imbalance? That is, were you unkind or perhaps just inattentive when your spouse really needed you to step up but you didn't or were too engaged elsewhere to notice?

4. If you were to write a "relational prescription" for a couple in precisely your situation of life to keep them growing together instead of apart, what would it be?

9

Naked and Unashamed

I slid into the restaurant booth first, and Lisa snuggled up next to me, giving a little exclamation of delight.

"Oh, are you cold?" asked the young woman sitting across from us.

"No," Lisa said. "He's just been gone all day. I haven't seen him yet. I miss him."

One of the most healing aspects of marriage for me has been the fact that I live with a woman who knows me better than anyone else ever has or ever will and yet—wonder of wonders—she still likes me. She even respects me. Even with all my particularities and weaknesses, she truly wants to be with me. That brings a lot of healing to a basically insecure man (and says some marvelous things about the graciousness of my wife).

Such an acceptance, however, requires one of the things most of us fear: honesty. We cannot be intimate with someone we are lying to. By definition, intimacy means being fully known and fully accepted. Your spouse can't "accept" what he or she doesn't know. In turn, you can't be accepted if you don't allow your spouse to get to know the real you.

It is wonderfully healing to be accepted and still loved when your spouse knows all your weaknesses. On the other hand, if you're keeping a secret, it's terrifying to think that one "disclosure" will end your spouse's affection and perhaps even lead to a divorce. There can be no peace if you live in perpetual fear of being "found out." Eventually, you will begin to resent rather than welcome your spouse's presence, and that is devastating to a marriage.

Sustaining your marriage on a lie is the opposite of the magnificent obsession because it requires you to push *out* Jesus, who said, "I am the way and the *truth* and the life" (John 14:6). Lying to your spouse as a strategy for keeping the marriage together is to base your marriage on the work of Satan, of whom Jesus said, "There is no truth in him. When he lies, he speaks his native language, for he is a liar and the father of lies" (John 8:44).

A Chance Passed Over

Rachelle knew something was going on with her husband. She had a sense he was keeping something from her, so she sat with him over coffee in a private place and said, "I am the kind of woman who will work through anything—and I mean *anything*—to save our marriage, but I need to know what it is."

With his wife having opened the door so wide, her husband confessed to one of his least offensive sins. When, months later, the truth of what he *could* have confessed came out, the marriage was over. He had broken his marital vows several times over with several people, and Rachelle told me she couldn't rebuild a marriage with a guy who had *never* been honest with her and still wasn't willing to be honest until forced to.

Guys, this isn't specific to men, but I hear it more commonly from the wives: they often fear what they don't know more than they would hurt over what they might find out. Here's what I hear:

"He won't let me in."

"I know something is going on, but he won't open up."

"I lie awake at night and imagine the worst."

We don't open up because we don't want to hurt our wives with what we've done or what we're struggling with, but our wives are often hurt more by our secrecy than they are by our disclosure. The only way forward is through increased honesty.

A Caveat

I'm not suggesting we become brutally frank to the point where we share secrets that serve no purpose other than to hurt our spouses, or that we are obligated to share things we know will do more harm than good. Counselors tell me they have heard people say things they know their spouses will never get over. I'm not talking about sharing things like that. What I am saying, however, is that we commit to live "in the light" with each other. We don't hide who we really are. And we certainly don't nurse and perpetuate addictions by covering them up.

If you're wondering what you should share, be thoughtful about how, when, and why you do that. Discuss with a licensed counselor, "Is this something I should share? If so, in what way and to what extent?"

Psychologist and author Juli Slattery told me:

> A wife fears rejection from her spouse, so she keeps secrets about struggles, fears, and mistakes. A husband would rather carry his own struggles rather than be vulnerable with his wife. These choices are not loving, but selfishly withholding. However, there are times when love compels us to measure our words. In

moments of anger and disappointment, the "truth" of how you might feel toward your spouse might be crushing and cruel. Sharing intimate details of sexual temptations and failings may deeply wound your spouse. Only by seeking the Lord's wisdom can we discern how to live authentically by sharing boldly while loving deeply.

If you think there is any chance a disclosure could be particularly painful to your spouse, please talk to a trusted, mature friend or pastor first. This person can then perhaps suggest a licensed counselor if he or she thinks you're correct in your assessment. You may well be encouraged to share *eventually*, but how and when you share is crucial. One wrong thing, shared in the wrong way and at the wrong time, can become a *lifelong* wound.

Finding a Way Forward

Justin Davis appeared to be a successful pastor and a loving husband and father, but he had a secret. He had been nursing an addiction to pornography for years. As sometimes happens with such struggles, the addiction spread beyond the digital world, and Justin had an affair with his wife's best friend.

Imagine Trisha's devastation: with one horrible disclosure she lost her pastor, her best friend, her husband, and the father of her children. In their excellent book, *Beyond Ordinary*, Justin and Trisha Davis tell the story of how repentance, forgiveness, a new commitment to honesty, and the presence of God helped them grow their way back together.

The part of Justin's testimony that hit me most is that he believes (if I understand him correctly) that deceit was a greater problem than lust. Deceit enabled the lust and allowed the lust to spread to an affair.

It enabled the sin to grow in the dark and remove natural boundaries. That's why Justin doesn't just focus on "purity" of mind in the sense of internet filters and the like, but also a *passionate pursuit of truth*.

He now regularly asks himself the following questions:

1. Is the fear of the consequences of the truth greater than my commitment to tell the truth?
2. Am I telling myself the truth?
3. Is there a truth I have distorted or am distorting right now?
4. Is there something I have withheld or am currently withholding from my spouse?[1]

In our pursuit of a more intimate union, are we living "naked and unashamed" or "covered up and very ashamed"? Are we revealing or hiding the essence of who we truly are? Are we harboring lies and covering them up with "verbal clothing"?

Being naked and unashamed means being able to tell your spouse about the real you—the innermost recesses of your soul. Maybe you need to tell your spouse you're having trouble at work rather than worrying that the situation might freak him or her out. Maybe you need to open up about the tenuous state of your finances. Or maybe it's a growing dependence on alcohol or food that's starting to scare you and you need someone to help you face this new challenge. Such conversations can be terrifying to consider, but they are the doorway to true intimacy.

Duplicity

Spiritually speaking, living a lie is living in duplicity. We're acting as if something is true when it's not. Duplicity severely undercuts our pursuit of holiness. On the one hand, the fear of being found out can keep us from making a poor choice (marital accountability at its best), but duplicity diabolically undermines this by presenting us with a twisted solution: "Here's the way to fulfill your desire: Do it, *but lie about it.* Then you can enjoy the desire *and* avoid the consequences." Duplicity says, "A second sin can help you enjoy the first sin," thus *multiplying* your sinful desires.

But honesty says, "You know that if you do this you will break your spouse's heart. You know the consequences will last much longer than the pleasure. You can't maintain an intimate marriage and keep this from your spouse, so why do it?" Honesty helps *crucify our sinful desires.*

A commitment to live in honesty
with my spouse is also a safeguard
in my walk with God.

Duplicity not only destroys marital intimacy; it also destroys our spiritual intimacy with God. Duplicity requires that we deaden ourselves (a horrific thought) to the loving voice of the Holy Spirit, who is warning us to turn around. The more we are intent on fulfilling the desire than on walking in truth, the more we have to train ourselves to shut out God's passionate and loving warnings.

Once we *start* falling from God, we quickly lose touch with how far we have fallen. The less sensitive we are to His voice, the less aware we are of His presence. That's a treacherous place to live. I have seen men and women reduced to mere shells of what they once were after cutting the tether of sensitivity toward the voice of God and losing their reverence for His commands. It's horrific, in every sense of the word.

So a commitment to live in honesty with my spouse is also a safeguard in my walk with God.

Courageous Love

The temptation to be dishonest isn't always to cover for our bad behavior; sometimes we're dishonest because we don't want to confront our spouses' bad behavior.

Franklin acted like a jerk at a dinner party, and someone publicly called him out on it. On the drive home, he asked his wife, "Do you think I was being a jerk?"

Sarah felt her heart race. She *did* think Franklin had acted like a jerk, but still she said, "No. Jason overreacted. You were just being honest."

This was a lost opportunity, and it enabled Franklin's future misbehavior.

Refusing to lovingly, honestly, and gently confront each other has kept many couples in a spiral of frustration. One woman couldn't bear to tell her husband that she wasn't very interested in sex because he smelled when he came to bed. She didn't want to hurt him—who wants to hear a spouse say he or she smells? But her lack of enthusiasm for sex over the course of two decades hurt him far more than if she had just been honest about his need to take a shower and brush his teeth.

If you are married to a supremely selfish wife and never raise the issue, in the end you enable her selfishness. Her friendships and her relationships with her children will suffer. Be courageous and love her with honesty.

Your spouse may not receive your truth. Once he or she knows your opinion and won't accept it, it's not duplicity to let it rest for a bit—you're just being pragmatic. Your spouse may not be ready to deal with it, and you can't force it. But the key is, *you're not pretending*, and your spouse knows it.

Do you truly desire marital intimacy, that blessed sense of being one? Embrace truth as a fundamental commitment in your life and marriage.

There are millionaires who would trade all their money and success for a middle-class life if only they could be naked and unashamed again, especially with their spouses. They know that attaining "success" while living in the dark isn't *truly* living. It's hiding, it's fearful, and it's lonely. The only way to be truly happy and successful in marriage is by living naked and unashamed.

Building a Lifelong Love

1. Does your spouse know all your weaknesses? Name one or two of your shortcomings that you can be grateful your spouse knows and can help you overcome.

2. What is your worst deceit in marriage, as you read this? What should your spouse know that he or she doesn't know? Whom can you talk to in order to consider whether this is something you need to share?

3. For many couples, an honest twenty-minute conversation once upon a time could have spared them twenty years of frustration. Is there an ongoing issue in your marriage that you've been afraid to bring up? Prayerfully consider how (and if) you should bring this up with your spouse.

4. What are two or three ways you can make your spouse feel more secure in your love so that he or she will feel more confident to be completely honest with you? Is there something you do or regularly say that might make your spouse feel legitimately fearful to "walk in the light" because of how you might react?

Blessed to Bless

One of the great challenges of marriage is that some of us want intimacy in the abstract more than we want it in reality. We want the *benefits* of being known and loved, but we hate the *process* of dying to ourselves that it takes to get there. We're a little like the people who want to become famous but then, once they become famous and must live with the hassles, wish they could become anonymous again. Some of us get married thinking we really want a life of intimacy, but once the challenges and burdens of intimacy press in on us, we want to go back to being selfish and estranged.

To enjoy the full benefits of marriage, a couple must start thinking like one, tackling every problem as one, taking care of each other as one. If a husband notices that his wife is getting too tired, working too hard, and not taking care of herself, that becomes *his* problem too. If a wife senses that her husband is discouraged, that discouragement becomes *her* discouragement too.

Becoming one with my spouse means I care as much about her problems as mine, that I cherish her health, her well-being, her pleasure as much as I cherish mine.

If I poison *my* mind with lust, I'm poisoning *our* marital bed. If I get reckless with *my* wallet, I'm putting *our* account at risk. In fact,

I can't do anything that won't affect my wife, so I want to not only watch out for her but to actively seek out and serve her well-being.

There can be no marital intimacy if two individuals refuse to die as individuals and be reborn as a couple.

Couples who have never pursued oneness like this don't truly know what marriage to each other is like. They're roommates, maybe even best friends, but they're not *married* in the fullest sense of the word. If you're disappointed in a disconnected marriage to your current spouse, that doesn't mean you'd be disappointed in a connected and intimate marriage to your current spouse. Instead of changing spouses, why not first try changing "disconnected" to "connected" and see how it goes? You've discovered that you loathe living together as mere roommates, but why not give intimate marriage a try?

Some of you are no doubt asking, "But *how*, Gary? *How* do we become one?" If you look back at the chapters in this section, you'll see we've already laid the groundwork: we have to employ *both* the supernatural and the science, we have to navigate the "power shifts" during the different seasons of marriage, and we have to be absolutely honest with each other.

Now we're going to look at three additional tools in this chapter. The first is learning to ask the right question.

The Tale of Two Questions

Every day I wake up and my "natural" (but sinful) man asks, *How can I get my needs met today?* Yet God wants me to respond "supernaturally" to each new day by asking a very different question—one that will lead to intimacy in marriage: *How can I bless my spouse today?*

Back in the time of Abraham, before Israel even existed, God chose an individual and made an amazing promise: "I will bless you ... so that you will be a blessing" (Gen. 12:2 NRSV).

In the New Testament, blessing others is a basic Christian practice: "Do not repay evil for evil or abuse for abuse; but, on the contrary, repay with a blessing. It is for this that you were called—that you might inherit a blessing" (1 Pet. 3:9 NRSV). Notice that Peter urges blessing even in the midst of conflict.

Because God has blessed me, I am to be a blessing to others. He has taken care of my greatest needs, so now I can focus on taking care of another's.

This brings us back to the two questions we can ask daily within marriage that will take us to two entirely different dimensions—intimacy or estrangement.

We can ask, "How can I bless you?"

Or we can ask, "How can I get my needs met?"

If I focus on the second question, every conflict will be resolved in terms of how I benefit from the outcome, even at my spouse's expense. That's thinking like an individual. But if I focus instead on the first question, every conflict will be resolved in terms of how my spouse is blessed in the process. That's thinking like we're one, and it leads to greater intimacy.

This approach is both spiritual *and* cognitive. I've got to pray that God will change my heart so that I truly desire to bless my spouse even if I'm disappointed in her, frustrated with her, or angry with her. And cognitively, I have to *choose* to look at every moment of marriage as an opportunity to purposefully bless my wife.

Most marital disagreements result from living in the second dimension and thinking as individuals. "What causes fights and quarrels among you?" James asks. "You covet but you cannot get what you want" (4:1–2). Instead of quarreling, I should ask myself, *What's the best way to bless my spouse in this situation?*

Does this mean we become "sacred doormats"? Absolutely not. It all depends on the content of the word *bless*.

For instance, in a real-life scenario, a husband told his wife, "Quit throwing away my pornography. I need it. If you throw away my pornography, I'm throwing away your Bible." The wife's desire is that her husband not keep a stash of pornography. That's what *she* wants, but it's *also* what will most bless her husband. So she doesn't give way and allow him to maintain a separate sexual life apart from their marital intimacy. She blesses him by saying, "No, I won't stand for this." Sometimes what we want can also be a blessing to our spouses, even if they don't want it. To bless other people is to seek their ultimate good, and their ultimate good is what draws them to God.

A husband might bless his wife by truly wanting her to consider a healthier lifestyle. He might want her to be released to enjoy sexual intimacy more freely and more often and have more energy for life in general. Of course, he would benefit from both these aims, but if he is driven by a desire to bless her and not to get what he wants, he will still be living to bless her.

Every time you enter a conflict, every morning when you feel that selfish heart start to chirp, every evening when you look back over the day and start to feel resentment, attack it with the first dimension. Ask yourself, *How can I bless my spouse, right here, right now?*

As a caveat, let me remind you that we must *be* blessed *to* bless. Living a life of blessing means keeping up on our spiritual intimacy with God. His affirmation and presence have a "spillover" effect in our hearts. If we don't get filled up with Him, though, we won't have any blessing to spill over onto our spouses.

Killing Spiders

When the spider dropped in front of me, I killed it.

Part of me hates doing this. Most spiders don't hurt anyone. In fact, they serve a good purpose—they kill other insects. Personally, I have nothing against spiders.

But they make webs, and they bother Lisa. She hates them.

So I kill the spiders.

Because I'm married to Lisa, I've made a prior commitment that her feelings outweigh mine on a lot of matters, and the killing of spiders is one of them. I don't rethink this commitment every time I see a spider. Because I'm married to Lisa, it's already decided: if I see a spider in the house, I kill it so she doesn't have to. If it's near an outside door, she's happy to let me push the spider over the threshold and simply evict it from the premises. But if it's hanging around in an inner room, that spider is history.

Let me apply this more broadly. If Lisa's dad had been an alcoholic (he certainly wasn't), I would kill all alcohol use in my life. I don't have a theological problem with alcohol, but that wouldn't matter. Out of love for Lisa, if she were sensitive toward the potential devastation of alcohol abuse, I wouldn't want her to worry. If she were to smell it on my breath or catch me walking with a slight alcohol-induced stumble, the horror of her childhood might come crashing back with a vengeance. Giving up alcohol wouldn't be about my rights or even what the Bible "allows"; it would be about making Lisa feel safe and close to me.

I have to *choose* to look at every

moment of marriage as an opportunity

to purposefully bless my wife.

Rae fell in love with a man passionately devoted to Christ. His faith drew her to him first and foremost—until he confessed that it really bothered him when she gathered with her friends to watch *The Bachelor*. "That show represents everything we don't believe," Curtis pointed out, "and it attacks practically everything we *do* believe." Because Curtis was in med school, they didn't have a lot of free time together, and he wanted what little time they did have to be shared doing something they could both enjoy.

Rae chose to give up what was one of her favorite pastimes so that she could join her husband in recreation they could *mutually* enjoy during an especially busy season in life.

Some of you might be thinking, *Hey, that's not fair! I like an occasional beer!*

Or, *I enjoy watching that show! Why should I give it up just because my spouse has a problem with it?*

Here's why: the lifelong blessing of an intimate oneness far exceeds the temporary pleasure of any individual pursuit. You wouldn't run if it made your knees feel like they were being stabbed by knives. Why? Because you're "one" with your own body, and you wouldn't intentionally hurt yourself. If I want to become one with my wife, I can't enjoy pleasure at her expense.

The pursuit of marital intimacy requires that we kill certain "spiders" that bug our spouses, *just because they bug our spouses*. Scripture may not prohibit these spiders, and enjoying them may not be inherently wrong. But if they cause our spouses pain, that's good enough reason to kill them. It's all part of becoming one.

What spider are you letting live that's killing your marital intimacy? Do you know what your spouse's spiders are? If you value intimacy, if you value truly becoming one, do the loving thing: hunt those spiders down and destroy them.

I Was Born for This!

If we live with a true blessing mentality, when troubles arise, we will adopt the attitude of Proverbs 17:17: "A friend loves at all times, and a brother is born for a time of adversity."

A good firefighter doesn't resent getting a call in the middle of the night; that's what he or she has been trained to do—put out fires. In the same way, if we believe we are "born" to bear our spouses' adversities, we'll be eager to rise to the challenge instead of resenting the intrusion. We must become "firefighters" to our spouses, eager to help at any moment.

Imagine a wife whose husband is suffering a long bout of unemployment or addiction, and she rises up to say, "I was *born* for this! I can love my man in the midst of this!"

Imagine a husband whose wife was sexually abused as a child, creating all sorts of challenges for them as a couple in the bedroom while she seeks to find freedom and healing, and the husband takes up this biblical challenge and proclaims, "I can do this! I can love this woman! I was *born* to do this!"

Remember, we approach each issue as a couple. If my left arm is broken, my right arm doesn't complain that it has to do all the work. My body is a unit, and when any part is lacking, another part steps up. That's the goal of a truly intimate marriage.

Instead of seeing a weakness or limitation as a point of frustration, instead of feeling sorry for ourselves, we let adversity call out and even showcase our commitment. A biblical friend doesn't love only in times of wealth, health, and success or on sunny days. A biblical friend loves at *all* times. So instead of feeling sorry for ourselves when our spouses hit a dry spell or when they are going through a difficult time, let's lace up our shoes a little tighter and remind ourselves, "Here we go: I was born for this, to love this person at all times, even in adversity."

I Am Yours

My prayer is that the day would come when the two of you can say to each other in the fullest sense of the words, "I am yours."

When you get back together after a long day at work and your wife drops her car keys, sighs, and says, "What a day," can you make the mental adjustment to care and say, "Tell me all about it"? If you learn to do this, what you're really saying to her is "I am yours. I belong to you. Right now, this moment, you matter more to me than anyone or anything else."

When either partner has sexual desires (not even needs, desires are enough), will each partner say to the other, "I am yours"?

When a family member has a crisis at a really inconvenient time—a work deadline, a scheduled trip to go hunting or run a marathon—will we hold our plans loosely and say to our concerned spouses, "I am yours"? Or will our actions say, "I am yours—after I am my boss's (or my hobby's or anything else's)"?

If your wife has a party she really wants to attend but you have a game you really want to watch; if your husband has a hobby you really don't enjoy but you see the pleasure it gives him when you're there supporting him; if your spouse is going through a season when he or she needs extra care—will you *still* say, "I am yours"?

On the day you got married, a roomful of people and your God heard you tell your spouse, "I am yours." To experience oneness at its fullest, we need to keep following through on that declaration every day and in every way.

Building a Lifelong Love

1. Does the notion of *oneness*—a very high level of intimacy—frighten you or make you eager to experience it? What do you think you need to do to welcome the thought of true marital intimacy in your life? What are some of your fears and concerns?

2. Consider your last disagreement as a couple. Was your attitude *How can I get my needs met?* or *How can I bless you?* Do you think it's realistic that the latter can become your default position?

3. Take a moment to think about some "spiders" you need to kill in order to become more intimately connected with your spouse. Remember, spiders don't have to be morally wrong—they might just be about your spouse's preferences. Is there a spider you can kill that will help the two of you become closer?

4. If a friend is "born for adversity," just like a firefighter is born to fight fires, what specifically, as this applies to your marriage, were you born for?

Part 3

The Journey toward Love

The Most Important Thing

There were many on my high school track team who hated doing intervals. Intervals are intense workouts at high speed and shorter distances designed to increase your anaerobic capacity and thus make you faster. Some of my teammates didn't mind the longer, slower runs, where they could tell stories and joke around. But to run intervals on the track in full sight of the coach? Not so much.

I liked doing intervals. They hurt physically, but they fed right into my latent OCD-ness. (I may never have been diagnosed with OCD, but I live in the neighborhood right next door to it.)

The reason intervals are essential for track athletes is that every footrace is all about running faster than your competition. In the end, that's all that matters. Whether you go fast for 100 meters or 26.2 miles, all that is judged is how quickly you finish the race. They don't add or deduct points for how you look in your uniform. They don't care whether you look like a gazelle or a gorilla when you run. The "style points" that gymnasts and figure skaters used to take into account would frustrate me because they're so subjective. I prefer the stark evaluation of running events: first one over the line wins.

Christian ethics have a similar "this is all that really matters" element. Every New Testament ethic—beginning with Jesus and running through Paul, Peter, and certainly John—exalts the importance of one thing, and one thing only: love.

Jesus called love for others an essential element of the greatest commandment (see Matt. 22:37–40). John said that if we don't love, we're not believers (see 1 John 4:7–8). Peter likewise saw love as the essential element of Christian being: "Now that you have purified your souls by your obedience to the truth so that you have genuine mutual love, love one another deeply from the heart" (1 Pet. 1:22 NRSV).

We like to focus on individual points of piety, the "dos and the don'ts," but the New Testament ethic puts piety on a level of "Are you loving others?" Christians are called to become people who excel at loving *deeply*, from the heart. And marriage can teach us to do just that.

According to Paul, if you pray and prophesy but don't love, you are nothing (see 1 Cor. 13:1–2). If you know the Bible better than your spouse or anyone in your church but you love others the least, you are the least mature believer in your marriage and in your church.

It's all about love.

Marriage is one of the most beneficial tools God created to help us learn how to love. And growing in a biblical understanding and practical application of love—added to the magnificent obsession and an intentional pursuit of oneness—is the third leg of the stool of a flourishing, lifelong marriage.

The first two legs were about *spiritual intimacy* and *relational intimacy*. I call this third leg *devotional intimacy*, though I've never heard anyone else speak of this aspect of marriage. It comes from my belief that our devotion to love directly impacts the way we view and treat our spouses. In other words, my relationship with "love" predates and impacts my relationship with my wife; so if I want to grow in loving my wife, I must first grow in understanding and then practice what it truly means to love—that is, "devotional intimacy."

Our Greatest Need

I hate the very concept of a spiderweb. A creepy-crawly arachnid spins a trap to imprison insects and hold them in place until the spider can kill and eat them. It's as brutal as it is clever, as gruesome as it is sly.

Erecting a trap to consume someone is the opposite of love, which calls us to sacrifice in order to serve someone (see John 15:13). Yet I've met many well-dressed and seemingly pious "spider spouses." They construct marital webs by attracting mates they think will meet their needs. They "feed" off their spouses whenever they are hungry (for approval, sex, support, finances). Spiders don't give to anyone. Rather, they spend their lives creating traps and feeding off anything they catch.

Some people, in retrospect, will blatantly confess to having married as a spider:

> "I knew he'd put me through medical school."
> "I couldn't wait to have sex, and she was willing to marry me."
> "My kids needed a dad, and he seemed like he'd be a good one."

"I needed to get out of my parents' house, and he was offering a quick exit. I thought this would get my parents off my back."

"I'm an addict, and she's a helper. I thought I'd eventually destroy myself if she wasn't watching me all the time."

It's easy for a person to slip into the spider's role, even after the wedding. It doesn't sound so evil to expect another person to live for us when we couch the relationship in romantic language. And the fact that the other person, in the throes of infatuation, *has* practically lived for us prior to the wedding gives us some reason to believe this is normal, so why should it ever end?

For Christians, however, our highest desire for our spouses should be to want them to seek first the kingdom of God and to love God with all their hearts, souls, minds, and strength. Seeking to consume a spouse in the name of "love" is a selfish lie.

If you are plotting to get something from your spouse, just know that you're acting like a spider. Certainly, there are legitimate needs in marriage, and it's not wrong to ask for them to be filled. But I can't let my needs define my marriage or become the focus of my day. I shouldn't spend more time plotting how I can manipulate my spouse to do what I want than I do praying to God about how I can love, serve, and support her. Jesus Himself taught that it is better to give than to receive (see Acts 20:35). It's okay to ask, but our focus, our plotting, and our passion should be on giving.

It was a horrific revelation for me one day when, as I prayed, I realized I was trying to turn Lisa into a "love Gary like he wants to be loved" machine. That sounds horribly awful and narcissistic, but we all have the potential to start viewing marriage like that if we stop pursuing biblical love.

It took me years to come to the realization that marriage is about loving, serving, encouraging, and helping, in large part because my own perspective on my greatest need was entirely different from God's thoughts on the matter. I had yet to discover just how revolutionary His instruction could be to a marriage: "Be imitators of God, therefore, as dearly loved children and live a life of love, just as Christ loved us and gave himself up for us as a fragrant offering and sacrifice to God" (Eph. 5:1–2 NIV, 1984 edition).

Why Did You Get Married?

Ask yourself a question, but pause before you answer it: *Why did I get married?*

When this question came to me in prayer, I was shocked at my answer. In God's presence, I couldn't hide from the truth. I got married for entirely selfish reasons. I thought I'd have a better life being married to Lisa than not being married to her (or being married to someone else). The way she looked, the way she acted, the way she thought, my view of her potential as a parent—these were all things I wanted. Selfishly so. Yeah, I was a spider spouse.

It was shocking for me to realize I had gotten married for primarily selfish reasons, especially because I now understand that God created marriage in part to *rid* me of my selfishness and pride, to teach me how to "live a life of love." On my wedding day, God and I were working toward two entirely different aims. I wanted to be loved, whereas God wanted me to learn how to love.

No one has challenged me when I suggest in front of large groups that virtually all of us get married for selfish reasons. It's human nature. Yet we have to get over this if we want to experience a sacred marriage. That begins with understanding our greatest need from God's perspective: learning how to love.

Unfailing Love

The Bible actually warns us that romantic love is more likely to disappoint than satisfy in the long run. The wisdom writer speaks a universal truth: "What a person desires is unfailing love" (Prov. 19:22). But then he admits how elusive that is: "Many claim to have unfailing love, but a faithful person who can find?" (Prov. 20:6).

In the end, there's only one place we'll find unfailing love, and it's not in marriage: "I [God] lavish unfailing love for a thousand generations on those who love me" (Exod. 20:6 NLT).

Infatuation can make us feel like we might have found unfailing love in a spouse, but eventually life will prove that a mere person can't love us like that. Then we feel cheated and misled.

God could not make Himself more clear:

He wants us to learn how to love.

From God's perspective, our greatest need isn't to be loved—not because we don't need to be loved, but in the same way that a person who has just feasted at Thanksgiving doesn't need to eat. God *has* loved, *is* loving, and *will* love us like we can never be loved by anyone else. We may not experience that love in a personal way if we are not making our relationship with God a priority, but it is there for the taking. Which means my greatest need—and your greatest need—isn't to be loved because that need has already been met by God. Our greatest need is to learn *how* to love.

That's the key behind Ephesians 5:1–2. Because we are God's "dearly loved children," our need to be loved has been met. And now we are to imitate God by "living a life of love" (I just love that phrase) as Christ loved us and gave Himself up for us. God has done (and is doing) His part—He has loved us, and He keeps loving us. And as dearly loved children, we can now focus on the all-important task of "living a life of love."

In Colossians 3:14, Paul writes, "Above all, clothe yourselves with love, which binds everything together in perfect harmony" (NRSV). Peter uses nearly the same language, demonstrating that this was a common teaching in the early church: "Above all, maintain constant love for one another, for love covers a multitude of sins" (1 Pet. 4:8 NRSV).

In his letter to the Corinthians, Paul couldn't have been more intense on this subject: "If I have prophetic powers, and understand all mysteries and all knowledge, and if I have all faith, so as to remove mountains, but do not have love, I am nothing. If I give away all my possessions, and if I hand over my body so that I may boast, but do not have love, I gain nothing" (1 Cor. 13:2–3 NRSV).

Love, love, love. Two different biblical authors saying, "Above all, love." Jesus declaring love an essential element of the greatest commandment. God could not make Himself more clear: He wants us to learn how to love.

Few things will be as revolutionary in your marriage as accepting that your greatest need isn't to be loved but to learn how to love—not love Hollywood-style but love the way Jesus loved, the way the apostle Paul defined love. I challenge anyone to study the biblical exaltation of love, the sacrificial definition of love, and the imperative to keep loving and then tell me, "Don't worry, Gary, I've got love down pat. I'm ready for the next lesson."

If I think my greatest need is to be loved yet I'm not being loved by my spouse as I think I need to be, I will eventually become bitter and resentful. But if I honestly believe that I need to learn how to love, if I aspire to live a life of love above all else, then *every day* provides ample opportunities for me to grow in that regard, which means I will appreciate my marriage more and more. How much I accept this to be my greatest need will determine in large part my overall satisfaction in marriage.

Show me a person who thinks his greatest need is to be loved, and I'll show you a person who often wonders if he married the wrong person. Show me a person who truly aspires to live a life of love, and I guarantee she is more contented in her marriage than the average spouse.

She Asked a Question

The ability to love isn't something we master—it's a journey we begin. Paul commends the Thessalonians because "the love of every one of you for one another *is increasing*" (2 Thess. 1:3 NRSV). I should be more loving today than I was five years ago and much more loving five years from now than I am today. I need to keep working at love, appreciating that my marriage is tailor-made to help me grow in my greatest area of need. *I won't value the opportunity, however, if I don't see it as a need.*

In her book *What's It Like to Be Married to Me?*, Linda Dillow tells the true story of a military wife whose husband served as a brigade surgeon in Iraq. When he received notice six months after being deployed that he was about to get a two-week leave, he emailed his wife, Krista, whose first thoughts were along the lines of *Fantastic! I've been a single mom for six months, but now is my chance to have someone watch the kids while I get my nails done and have lunch with Becca.*

That was her initial inclination, but it was not the final one. She found herself praying, "How can I fill up my husband's spirit, soul, and body so that he can go back to war for six more months?" This was just another way of asking, *What if my greatest need isn't to be loved but to learn how to love? How would that affect this situation?*

God gave her some very practical ideas in answer to her prayer:

- She wrote Caleb and asked him everything he wanted to eat for two weeks.
- She bought seven "bedroom outfits" in seven different colors.
- She arranged childcare with a friend so she and Caleb could have twenty-four hours alone with each other.
- She bought a massage book and studied it.

After greeting Caleb at the airport, she and the kids took him out to dinner. Krista then made sure the kids were taken care of and, knowing that Caleb's love language was physical touch, they "made out—just because we could!"

She then went into the bathroom and drew Caleb a bath. The account is so touching, I'll let her describe it in her own words:

> I straddled the tub with my big sponge and began to
> cleanse the smells of war. And as I washed the odor
> of war away, I prayed to cleanse his soul from the
> spirit of death and destruction. As I washed his head

and hair, I prayed, *Lord, let nothing he has thought harm him.* As I wiped his eyes, I prayed, *Lord, let nothing he has seen stay in his heart.* As I washed his ears, I prayed, *Lord, let nothing he has heard touch his spirit.* I washed and prayed over every part of my husband, begging God that nothing would take root, that all evil would be washed away.

This was a very spiritual moment, literally praying for and all but anointing every part of her husband's body, pleading with God to bring healing and restoration. A very spiritual moment indeed.

Then it became very physical.

Krista climbed into the bath with him and said, "Honey, pick a color."

Caleb was confused. "Why?"

"Just pick one ... you'll be glad you did."

Caleb finally chose one, and Krista climbed out of the tub and in just a few moments came back into the bathroom wearing one of the bedroom outfits that was exactly the color Caleb had chosen. In Krista's words, "We made love five times in the first twenty-four hours he was home.... Was this even physically possible?" (I'm not sure. That may take military training.)

A few days later, Krista put her new massage techniques into practice. Caleb became so relaxed during the massage that he slept for two hours straight and woke up saying, "That was amazing. I never slept like that once in Iraq."

Caleb did offer Krista some time to catch up on things. She got to go to the salon and she did get a nice, long lunch with Becca. But her focus was on her husband—which seems astonishing to me. I get how a young mother raising kids on her own would want to take advantage of her spouse being home. But looking at her greatest need through this new lens created an experience I think most wives would consider "legendary." Just listen to her description: "Our two weeks were a supernatural feast of intimacy with the Lord and with one another."

Is there a wife alive who wouldn't want to know the doorway to a "supernatural feast of intimacy"? This is such an amazing expression, even more surprising in that it was born out of service, humility, and generosity instead of cleverness, sexual gimmicks, and selfish demands.

Krista went on. "Had I loved him, spirit, soul, and body, so he was ready to return to war? Three days after he got back, he emailed me and said, 'Thank you for the best two weeks of my life.'"[1]

Once again, let me reiterate that I can imagine that any woman in Krista's situation would think, *Now it's my turn. Finally, I get a break. Now someone takes care of me.* But Krista didn't choose the natural; she chose the supernatural. She brought God into her marriage by asking how *she* could love instead of focusing on how she wanted to *be* loved, and the results were "a supernatural feast of intimacy."

Will you accept that your greatest need—unfailing love—can be met completely only by God? And will you then accept that your greatest need now, with the comfort of that love, is to learn how to love?

If you will, I believe your marriage will take you to a depth of spiritual intimacy and satisfaction that is unrivaled.

"I give you a new commandment, that you love one another. Just as I have loved you, you also should love one another. By this everyone will know that you are my disciples, if you have love for one another" (John 13:34–35 NRSV).

Building a Lifelong Love

1. What was your primary motivation for getting married? How has believing that your primary need is to be loved affected your satisfaction in marriage? In what ways has it made life difficult for your spouse?

2. Have you ever consciously thought about improving in the art of "living a life of love?" Name two things you think you need to begin doing on that journey.

3. Think of a situation in your marriage right now where you can easily be stretched to love in a way you never have before. Will you accept the challenge, pray about your heart and actions, and grow accordingly?

4. How can you become a Krista to your spouse in whatever he or she is going through?

Absolute Benevolence

What causes you to love your spouse?

Is it her grace?

His kindness?

Her strength?

His humor?

Here's the catch: If you love your spouse because she is kind, you love kindness, not your spouse. If you love your spouse because he is thoughtful, you love thoughtfulness, not your spouse.

True love is found in *absolute benevolence*, a state of the heart that is bent toward being devoted to someone's highest good, regardless of that person's actions or character. Absolute benevolence is a disposition to do what is best for the other, out of the inner compulsion from the Holy Spirit, to serve this person's best interests.

Christ died for us while we were yet sinners (see Rom. 5:8). He didn't love us because we were obedient or kind or thoughtful. He loved us with an absolute benevolence that will sound like a tautology: He loved us because He loves us. There is no explanation for this love. Someone objectively examining it could only conclude, "Why did God choose to love *him*? Why does God choose to love *her*? It makes no sense."

What this means, men, is that when I'm called to love my wife as Christ loves the church (see Eph. 5:25), I'm called to love her with absolute benevolence. To model such a love, we need to love so benevolently that onlookers might say, "Wow, he really loves her. Why would a man love a woman *that much*?"

As married people, we are invited to adopt an attitude of absolute benevolence toward our spouses, which means always wanting what is best for them. Love is always set on the beloved's welfare, so all our actions should be motivated for their good. *All* our actions. Every one.

How do we get there? Is this even realistic?

> If we're not worshipping God daily
> to receive His absolute benevolence,
> we'll soon run out of our own.

Big attitudes can be shaped through little actions. When we were visiting the Seattle area one Thanksgiving, it was—surprise, surprise—raining hard. Lisa grew up in the Pacific Northwest and is used to the wet, but she's been in Houston for years now and has become less comfortable with rain. My only thought was to get her from our car and into my parents' house as quickly as possible and as dry as possible. I got out of the car and opened up the back to get my suitcase, then closed it.

Lisa was a couple of steps behind me. "If you open it back up, I can get mine," she said. Lisa hates moving suitcases; she was just being kind.

"Don't worry. I've got it," I said. "Besides, it's raining."

"But that means you'll have to go out in the rain *twice* to bring in mine."

What she was saying was logical, but I was looking at the situation, at least in one sense, biblically. There are a thousand and one ways I could improve on being a husband, but in this instance my concern really was solely focused on Lisa and how I could best serve her. She doesn't like to handle suitcases, and she's not a fan of getting her hair wet before a family dinner. How long I was going to be in the rain wasn't even on my radar. I just didn't want her to have to do something I know she really doesn't like to do.

That's a small, insignificant example, but small moments can become habits, and habits shape character. If we aspire to true love for our spouses, then we have to look at such everyday situations and ask ourselves, *How can I bless my spouse here?* A disposition to always do what is best for the other, out of the inner compulsion from the Holy Spirit, is absolute benevolence.

Prevailing Love

"Absolute benevolence" is another way of describing *prevailing* love, or *lifelong* love. If I love my spouse because I love my spouse, I don't love her because she's healthy or young or beautiful or wealthy or godly or because she has given me a family. So I won't stop loving her if she grows sick or old or becomes disfigured or gets in debt or rebels against God. I'll love her because I love her.

Since marriage calls us to absolute benevolence, which is an *unconditional* commitment, it requires nothing less than the presence of God, the only true source of such love.

Think about it: Who lovingly preaches to people whom He knows just want to trap Him into saying something for which they can kill Him?

Jesus.

Who devotes Himself radically and sacrificially to a group of men who will desert Him just when He needs them most?

Jesus.

Who prays for those who are crucifying Him?

Jesus.

Who dies for someone who has rebelled against Him?

Jesus.

Absolute benevolence is born not just by trying harder but rather by going to God, receiving His love and passing it on, and letting Him transform us so that we love because He first loved us. If we're not worshipping God daily to receive His absolute benevolence, we'll soon run out of our own. We just can't love this way in our own strength.

A Loving Hand Is a Strong Hand

Now, absolute benevolence does not mean you let your spouse run all over you. I received an email from a wife asking how to respond when her husband says that part of "accepting" him is accepting that he is an alcoholic and is going to get drunk. Love does not stand by while another person ruins himself.

After all, God loves us—and disciplines us. "When we are judged in this way by the Lord, we are being disciplined so that we will not be finally condemned with the world" (1 Cor. 11:32). God would rather see us walk through shame, pain, the loss of a job, and even worldly humiliation on our way to heaven than to watch us walk comfortably into hell. He disciplines us for our own good.

A husband and wife I talked to were being ground down by the wife's poorly chosen priorities. The husband had put up with it for too long, and his bitterness was palpable. He thought love meant just grinning and bearing it, but that's a short-term strategy at best. The most loving thing he could do was what he eventually did—bring the two of them to a counselor's office where these issues could be addressed. She had a couple of hobbies and a proclivity toward spending time on social media at the expense of their young children. She wanted to be cherished by her husband, but she needed to see that one of the things that would help him cherish her was being willing to reassess her priorities. The Bible describes Christ's love for the church—as an example to husbands—as serving her sanctification, or growth in holiness (see Eph. 5:25–27).

Absolute benevolence is the proper passion behind every marital action. If I must separate from my spouse, I will do it, but only because it must be best for her. This is true in cases of abuse. Wives, it's best for your husbands not to hit you, so if the only way you can stop them from doing that is to remove yourselves from their presence, that's what you do. But even that act, from that disposition, is absolute benevolence (though a selfish man will accuse you otherwise).*

This means that to find the right way to act, I must ask, from God's perspective, What is truly best for my spouse? The answer to this question tells me what I must will myself to do.

---

* Please read the appendix for an important word about the church's response to domestic violence.

Let me assure you, the more you pursue absolute benevolence, the more your love for your spouse will be renewed. When I love my wife with absolute benevolence, just the sound of her name or the mere thought of her smile moves me in a way that is difficult to explain. Our hearts will follow our actions.

Building a Lifelong Love

1. List several of your favorite things about your spouse. Thank God that He has given you someone with these qualities.

2. This is going to seem a bit artificial, but I believe you will find it helpful. Rate your love for your spouse on a scale from 1 to 10, with 1 meaning you love your spouse mostly for what he or she brings to your life and who he or she is, and 10 meaning you believe you are loving your spouse with absolute benevolence. (I don't expect to hear of any 10s.) Now, sit before God with your answer, and let Him lead the conversation about how you can begin loving your spouse with the same love with which He loves you.

3. Is it realistic to expect yourself to have an attitude of absolute benevolence toward your spouse, meaning your every action is motivated for the good of him or her? Why does such unconditional commitment in a marriage require nothing less than the presence of God?

4. Think of three small things you would have done differently in just the past twenty-four hours if you had been seeking your spouse's highest good. What do you think it might do to the way you think and feel about your marriage when you pursue the kind of love found in absolute benevolence?

13

Love Most Famous

First Corinthians 13 is one of the most famous chapters in the Bible, and rightly so, as it brilliantly defines biblical love. Let's consider just one simple phrase from the passage, "Love does not boast," and apply that to marriage.

Javier complains, "Contrary to stereotype, I'm by far the most romantic partner in our relationship. I spend months thinking about birthday, anniversary, and Christmas presents. I surprise my wife with flowers and her favorite candy just because. But Martina feels like she nails it if she just gives me a *card*, and most often it's 'Your present is still coming, but it's in the mail.' And guess what the mail never delivers?"

I'm not saying Javier doesn't have a legitimate complaint; clearly, Martina seems to be taking him for granted. But Javier is in spiritual danger if he begins defining their entire relationship by one thing he does well that his wife does poorly—giving gifts—especially since he has a habit of telling all their friends about this dynamic. I pointed out to Javier that the Bible says, "Love doesn't boast." If Javier wants to pursue biblical love instead of a "You scratch my back and I'll scratch yours" love, he needs to realize that boasting of how he excels as a husband isn't love; it's prideful competition.

Paul also tells us that "love keeps no record of wrongs." Yet one wife told me, "When my husband was eighteen, he got fired from Taco Bell for being habitually late. When he was twenty-four, he got kicked out of college for never completing his final course. When he turned thirty, he lost his job because he kept forgetting to answer his phone and was missing too many calls. He's been messing up his whole life."

I'm sure this must be extremely frustrating, but if this wife wants to love biblically, she must remember that love "keeps no record of wrongs." Where does the Bible say, "Love your husband *unless he loses a job in college, gets kicked out of college, and is fired for being absentminded*"? I must have missed that verse.

Both of these marriages have legitimate issues to address. I agree with both spouses on that. I am *not* excusing such behavior or failings. But what these spouses were blind to was the state of their own hearts and God's astonishing, radical definition of love, which requires us to be so *for* someone—in the way that God is for us in Romans 8:31—that it almost sounds absurd. We must become our spouses' biggest *champions* despite their faults, even as God is *our* biggest champion despite *our* faults. "God proves his love for us in that while we still were sinners Christ died for us" (Rom. 5:8 NRSV).

All too often we like to use a spouse's failure as a reason to stop loving, whereas the Bible calls us to do exactly the reverse: apply love exactly where and when our spouses mess up. That doesn't mean ignoring bad behavior or avoiding legitimate consequences, but it does mean guarding our hearts from pride, resentment, and bitterness.

Just because we can "prove" our spouses have "issues" does not mean we should be focused on our spouses' failings instead of our own heart issues. When I call people out on this attitude using 1 Corinthians 13 to define what love is and isn't, they are usually stunned. "I never thought of it like that," they say. Spiritually, they're completely numb to conviction over their biblically described offense to love, yet if any of them suffers a lack of feelings for any significant season, they panic and think something is wrong with their marriages.

If you truly want a lifelong love, then you must first accept the biblical definition of what love actually is. And it has nothing to do with how you feel.

Sadly, most people are more appalled by their lack of feelings for a spouse than they are that their own actions directly contradict what the Bible defines as loving. If you truly want a lifelong love, and I hope you do, then you must first accept the biblical definition of what love actually is. And it has nothing to do with how you feel.

To that end, let's go through Paul's list in 1 Corinthians 13:4–8 (NASB, 1995 edition), and ask yourself, *Is this how I love in my marriage?* Remember, you are not evaluating your spouse here because you're not responsible for your spouse's actions in this sense.

LOVE IS PATIENT.

Lisa and I were once driven around Charlotte by a wonderful couple, Lloyd and Pam Bustard. Lloyd is a multiply gifted man—a preacher, pastor, and musician—but he couldn't seem to drive two city blocks without taking a wrong turn. Yet his wife, Pam, displayed the most astonishing patience, without any irritation in her voice, that Lisa and I had ever seen. "No, babe, you took a wrong turn there. We have to do a U-turn and go back."

"But I think it's up here."

"No, it's back there."

"Oh, you're right."

There was no consternation in Pam's voice. No condescension. Not even a hint of any lack of respect. Multiple mistakes didn't seem to irritate her. Pam just sat next to Lloyd and loved him the way 1 Corinthians 13 calls us to love. And we could tell she had been doing this for years.

Do you treat your spouse's limitations like Pam treats Lloyd's?

LOVE IS KIND.

What have you done for your spouse lately? If you were to list your acts of kindness over the last seven days, how long (or short) would the list be? Have you seen a need and sought to meet it? Have you considered what active thing you could do for your spouse to demonstrate your love and care? If you spend more time evaluating whether or not you still feel like you're "in love" with your spouse than you do plotting to do kind deeds for your spouse, you've traded the Bible's definition of love for the world's.

LOVE IS NOT JEALOUS.

Do you resent that your spouse gets more consideration from his or her spouse (that is, from you) than you get from yours (that is, from him or her)? That's jealousy! This may sound weird, but I've found it to be relatively common for spouses to wish they got treated the way they treat their spouses. In a spiritual quirk, they are jealous of their own treatment.

Do you resent that your spouse's role in the family seems easier or better than yours at times? That's jealousy. Real love would be gratified that our spouses have it "better" than we do. Knowing this would delight us rather than make us feel resentful, if our hearts were filled with biblical love.

LOVE DOES NOT BRAG AND IS NOT ARROGANT.

How often do you think you're the "better" spouse? That attitude will keep you from excelling and growing in love and instead foster bitterness and resentment. Love would never say, "I do this for you, and that for you. I keep on doing x, y, and z, and what do you ever do for me?"

What did the disciples ever give to Jesus? How did they give back to Him, proportionally speaking? Would Jesus ever say, "I do miracles for you, I feed you, I pray for you, I teach you all day long. I'm even going to die for you, so what are you going to do for Me?" Remember, we are called to love like Jesus loves.

LOVE DOES NOT ACT UNBECOMINGLY.

This essentially means being rude. How often do you respond to your spouse with sarcastic words and attitudes? How do you treat him or her in public—is your goal to make people pity you for having such a difficult spouse, or is it to proclaim that you treasure your spouse? God treasures you, with all your weaknesses and even your sins. He delights in you. And your sins, which are known to God, vastly outnumber the sins you are aware of in your spouse. God doesn't act rudely toward us, despite knowing all that He knows. Will we act rudely to our spouses, knowing what little we know?

LOVE DOES NOT SEEK ITS OWN.

Be careful about demanding that your spouse speak your love language or meet your need for love and respect. Helpful tools designed to teach us how to love our spouses can be turned around (against the authors' intentions) and used as weapons to accuse our spouses for how they are not measuring up.

LOVE IS NOT PROVOKED.

Biblical love isn't irritable. It doesn't lash out at the least bit of provocation. Rather, it remains calm and gentle and tries to be understanding. It injects calm and collectedness into every situation. It looks out for the triggers of an impending, hurtful argument and says, "I'm not going to take the bait. I'm going to breathe deeply and remain grounded."

LOVE DOES NOT TAKE INTO ACCOUNT A WRONG SUFFERED.

Does your spouse routinely receive grace or judgment from you? Is he or she built up with acceptance or weighed down with your disappointment? Is your spouse frequently reminded of how he or she never lives up to your expectations? One goal of biblical love should be that our spouses are far more aware of what we like about them than they are of what they do that frustrates us.

LOVE DOES NOT REJOICE IN UNRIGHTEOUSNESS, BUT REJOICES WITH THE TRUTH.

When you and your spouse disagree, are you more concerned about addressing your contribution to what's wrong or about being proven right? Seek the truth rather than vindication. This also means, however, that when a spouse wants to do something sexually that another spouse has a moral problem with, biblical love doesn't just give in. If a spouse is committing fraud, alienating a child, or ruining his or her life, love doesn't mean playing nice and pretending that all is well. Love is strong and courageous and speaks what is true, not always what will please.

LOVE BEARS ALL THINGS.

This means we're called to bear not just some of our spouses' weaknesses but all of them. *All* of them. That's right—the one that just came into your mind and made you say, "Are you serious?" Yes, I am. That one.

LOVE BELIEVES ALL THINGS AND HOPES ALL THINGS.

Do you have hope that your spouse can become all that God created him or her to be? Or have you stopped believing for your spouse? Do you still dream that God can be fully known and revealed in your spouse's life? Or have you given up hope to the extent that you tell your spouse you know he or she is just going to fail again? To give up hope in your spouse is to give up hope *in God* and His ability to change someone's heart. It's a monstrous thing to do.

LOVE ENDURES ALL THINGS.

There's that phrase "all things" again. Love endures *all* things.*
Whatever my spouse puts me through, whatever life leads me
through, my call to love is a call to endure. Here *endures* assumes
that the problem is ongoing and isn't immediately fixed. *All things*
means that, whatever the ongoing challenge, my goal is to build a
marriage worthy of my calling. If I'm running a marathon and it
starts to rain, I endure the rain. If there are hills, I endure the hills.
If it gets hot and humid, I endure the heat and humidity. If my legs
cramp, I endure the cramps. Whatever it takes to get to the finish
line, that's what I endure. That's biblical love in marriage.

LOVE NEVER FAILS.

Our spouses may not change; the Bible doesn't promise that everything will be "fixed" in the here and now. For our part, we can only
make sure our *love* doesn't fail. If you are married to a habitually
unfaithful spouse, a drug addict, someone who gets physically violent, or a spouse who is mentally ill and refuses to take medication,
your marriage may not survive. But that doesn't mean your love has
failed. You can keep loving your spouse, as Christ loves us, even as
your spouse destroys your marriage. In the end, you may have to let
your spouse go, as Christ lets rebellious sinners go. But that isn't a
failure of love—it's an expression of love.

Notice not once does the Bible say, "Love *feels* intensely." Let's
stop worrying about how we feel and start considering how we love:
Jesus-style. If we honestly measure our hearts by the truth of this

---

* This is *not* to suggest that you put up with ongoing unfaithfulness or abuse. We've talked elsewhere about how love confronts evil rather than enables it, so we have to allow one Scripture to
qualify another.

passage, we won't have time to worry about feelings. We'll be consumed with building a life of substance.

Pulling Tubes

Having just heard me speak on marriage, the sixty-something woman was already in tears by the time she inched to the front of the line. She had a story to tell, and she kept wiping away the tears until she could tell it.

"What you're saying is so true," she began and then paused to contain herself. "I've worked at a hospice for twenty years. Caring for people is what I do. Yet somehow, it never got transferred to home. I resented doing the very things for my husband that I spent my whole day doing for others." After another pause, she went on. "Until, that is, my husband got cancer. After the first operation, he stayed home for six weeks, and I stayed with him. It was the best season of marriage we've ever had."

Think about this: When describing "the best season of marriage we've ever had," she didn't choose the honeymoon, their young years when they were strong and vibrant, the exciting years when occupations opened up, the tired-but-thrilling years when the kids arrived. She had many highlights to choose from, yet this woman chose the season of her husband's *cancer* as the best season of marriage they had ever had.

Why?

"Pulling tubes, cleaning sutures—I'm a nurse, I can do all that—I finally began doing for him everything I've done for everyone else. But I had never served my husband like that the entire time we were married. But now I was. It changed my heart. It changed the way I looked at him. And serving him like that—it just drew us so close together."

Most people think their marriages will improve if their spouses step up. This wife said her marriage improved when *she* stepped up. I've never read a marital book that talks about building romance by pulling medical tubes and cleaning sutures on your partner, but this dear woman had stumbled onto a powerful truth. She entered into love, Jesus-style, and she passionately proclaims that it's a glorious love indeed.

Are you serving others more than you serve your spouse? Husbands, it goes without saying here that any sense of chauvinism, any sense that your wives are there primarily to serve you, goes completely against the spirit of biblical love. When Paul said to love our wives like Christ loves the church, he was calling us to be the leaders in service, not the leaders in privilege. Are you leading like that? And wives, do you find yourselves offering nurturing care to others outside the home with a sweet spirit but resenting it when providing similar care at your own address?

Changing the Goal

Many couples I talk to think the goal of marriage is to keep desiring each other like they did when they were infatuated. Now, sometimes I do still desire my wife with that intensity, but the constant goal I must really strive for is best expressed by the apostle John: "If we love one another, God lives in us and his love is made complete in us" (1 John 4:12).

You see, God's love isn't made complete in us or in our marriages when we just receive His love; it's made complete when we receive His love and pass it on to our spouses. *That's* what will sustain a marriage. Love is about far more than human desire. It is, quite literally, worship (acknowledging and reveling in His excellence) and surrender (giving way to His presence). Infatuation is much too small an aim!

The biblical goal of marriage is thus a shared experience of *God living in us and God's love being made complete in us.* The pursuit of a sacred marriage is the pursuit of God in marriage—seeking to experience His love (not our desire), His presence (not our happiness), and His glory (not our selfishness).

To the spiritually blind, this sounds ridiculously absurd. But those who have tasted God's goodness know that His love overwhelms our own desire, that His presence brings a joy that makes human "happiness" feel like a small shudder in the face of God's earthquake, and that His glory is so much more fulfilling, in every possible way, than our small-minded selfishness.

Here's the trap sacred marriage saves us from: if what you desire can never satisfy, you will never be satisfied, even if you obtain your desire. The world is teeming with disappointed souls who thought they had found their "one true love" and then one day woke up to find that their one true love wasn't very loving for very long. But if you place your hope in God's love, "hope does not disappoint us, because God's love has been poured into our hearts through the Holy Spirit that has been given to us" (Rom. 5:5 NRSV).

We can't sustain desire, but the Bible promises us that God will sustain *love* by continually pouring it into our hearts through His Holy Spirit. A marriage based on desire is like living on a floodplain—sometimes you'll be underwater, and sometimes it'll be bone dry. That's where, quite frankly, most couples exist. On the other hand, a marriage based on God's love is a steady mountain stream that will never run out.

Now, a trickier question: How does defining love this way relate to sexual desire? That question deserves a chapter all its own, which we'll turn to next.

Building a Lifelong Love

1. When you think about the state of your marriage, which are you more likely to evaluate—how you feel about your spouse, or how well your love matches up with the Bible's definition of love? What do you need to do to shift your thinking toward being more concerned about pursuing biblical love?

2. Is it possible for a person to take advantage of his or his spouse who tries to love according to I Corinthians 13? If so, what would be the spouse's most biblical response?

3. Go back over Paul's list in I Corinthians 13:4–8. Pick two things you think you need to focus on in the coming weeks.

4. One woman's love was renewed when she began "pulling tubes" for her sick husband. Are there any "tubes" you need to pull in your own marriage—acts of service you've perhaps done for others but have failed to do for your spouse? Sit before the Lord and invite His conviction.

Delightful Desire

The God of love (1 John 4:7) is the God who created sex. When we learn to make love the focus of sex in marriage, we embrace a powerful tool of healing, togetherness, and personal affirmation that enhances pleasure and relationship connection.

This might sound odd, but after the newness of sexual intimacy wore off, there came a time in my life when I resented the powerful force of sexual desire because of how vulnerable it made me to my wife.

In prayer, I even offered up this aspect of my free will. I thought perhaps God could cut me a break and magically reprogram my soul so that sexual desire would be much tamer, more focused, more easily controlled.

God gently reprimanded me. You see, I was looking at sexual desire through the lens of the fall, as if it came about because of Satan and sin. Intellectually, I would have rejected that notion. But in my fears, that's how it sometimes felt—that sexual desire was a temptation rather than a tool.

When I began looking at sexual desire through the lens of creation instead of the fall—grasping that it's there by God's design and therefore must have a God-honoring purpose—I realized that it is God's providential will that I be this vulnerable in my relationship with my wife. God knows that without sexual longing, I might grow weaker in my affections for His daughter. I might allow us to slowly drift apart without a barometer in the relationship to show me just how far we've drifted, until one day we wake up and can't even see each other over the horizon. God loves His daughter (and His son) too much to let that happen, so He designed me with hormones that will all but begin to roar if I slumber in my apathy toward my wife.

When I finally realized that God created me to desire my wife and to be vulnerable in that desire, I never looked at our sexual relationship in quite the same way. Sexual desire helps me keep the importance of our relationship (on all levels) in the forefront of my mind. A lifelong love is thus served, reinforced, and nurtured by lifelong sexuality.

The Desire That Heals

Done well, marital sexuality can be a supremely healing experience.

Most of us grow up with various insecurities about our bodies, and the thought that we are wanted, desired, enjoyed, and then pursued sexually (for the right reasons) can do wonders for a beaten-up self-image.

In the Song of Songs, written at a time in history when no woman would pay to get a tan (because in that day and culture, the lighter the better), an ashamed bride implored her friends, "Don't stare at me because I am dark—the sun has darkened my skin. My brothers were angry with me; they forced me to care for their vineyards, so I couldn't care for myself" (Song 1:6 NLT).

Today, millions of women pay good money to make their skin darker because it is widely perceived as more beautiful, not less. But this young woman feared that people were staring at her not because they were impressed but because they couldn't believe she'd let the sun darken her skin. Though she had entered marriage with an image of herself as attracting attention for all the wrong reasons, her husband set her straight: "How beautiful you are, my darling, how beautiful you are! … Like a lily among the thorns, so is my darling among the young women" (Song 1:15; 2:2 NASB).

Understanding this passage can reset a man's view of sexuality within marriage. If you cultivated your sexual interest with pornography, you got the idea that sex is all about getting to your own climax. But here it's all about affirming a woman who grew up believing she was lacking something significant in the beauty department. Though others had mocked her, and though she wasn't "classically" beautiful according to the standards of her culture, her husband not only considered her beautiful but the "*most* beautiful among women" (Song 1:8 NASB)

Whether it's about a woman's skin, hair, or shape or a man's *lack* thereof, cultural notions about what is beautiful and desirable make a million people feel shame for every one person who feels proud about her or his looks. And in the context of a *lifelong* love, artificial notions about what is truly beautiful are eventually obliterated by age.

Men, when we stop desiring our wives or start desiring other women, marital sexuality becomes yet another chapter in a woman's mental memoir where she thinks that she doesn't quite measure up. One of the most biblical reasons to guard our hearts and not let our desire for sexual relations fade (when it's physically possible to sustain) is to continue the healing process of our wives' images of themselves as beautiful, desirable women, whether they are twenty-nine, forty-nine, or sixty-nine.

And wives, the vast majority of men don't view your refusal of sexual intimacy as the refusal of an *act* as much as they experience it as a refusal of *them* and their desirability.

We won't go far wrong if we think of sexuality like this (wives, just switch the gender): "My wife has been hurt her entire life by an insane culture with ridiculous standards of physical beauty that make no sense. In the shelter of our marriage and under the covering of my love, I'm going to work overtime to affirm her, adore her, desire her, pursue her, verbally praise her, and bring healing to her soul. I want to desire her and love her so much that the hurts, taunts, and criticisms of others will become all but invisible in the force of my passion."

Sexual desire isn't just about our sexual needs; it's also about our spouses' hurting souls—using our desires to serve theirs. It's about letting our spouses relish and even cherish the power their beauty has over us: "You have enchanted my heart with a single glance of your eyes" (Song 4:9 NASB). It's about the confidence our wives gain when they know they have captured not just our hearts but our eyes and minds as well.

This is a tremendous gift, one a man gives by intention when he guards his heart, mind, and eyes and cultivates (or recultivates, if he has strayed) a singular attraction to the woman he calls "wife."

Of course, desire may not be a problem on the wedding night. But what about ten years or even twenty-five years into the marriage? How does desire fit into a *lifelong* love?

Keeping the Canary Alive

"Gary," the young wife explained to me, "I want to have a rocking sex life with my husband, but he criticizes everything I do. I don't cook right. I don't drive right. I don't raise the kids right. So I know he's also criticizing every move I make in the bedroom. I just can't bear to have another aspect of marriage life where I'm messing up."

This wife wants a great (rocking!) sex life, but she's tired of being criticized. Her coldness toward the marital bed has nothing to do with sex—it has everything to do with what happens *outside* the bedroom. Her husband won't warm her up by buying a sexual toy, trying out a new move, and certainly not by quoting 1 Corinthians 7. He has to address the relational poison that's killing her desire for physical passion. To put it bluntly, his wife hates being criticized more than she desires having an orgasm.

I look at a lack of sexual desire (except in cases where physical causes need to be addressed) as that famous "canary in the mine." Old-time miners used to keep canaries down in the depths of the mines. The tiny birds' lungs were so small that if relatively odorless poisonous gas were to seep out of the ground, the canaries would die first, thus warning the miners to get out of the shaft and into fresh air. In the same way, when sexual desire dies, absent physical causes, it's often indicative that there are relational "poisons" in the home. These toxins may not have killed the marriage yet, but they're making it sick, and the couple needs fresh air.

Sex is an easy measuring stick. If you ask a couple, "When was the last time you made love?" and they don't know, that's a big tell.

The early days of sexual passion are often easy, just as "feeling in love" is easy when we're infatuated. Sexual chemistry is plentiful, everything is new, and you can't get enough of each other. But maintaining this sexual interest is another challenge altogether. I've heard many times the cliché that if a married couple puts a marble in a jar every time they have sex for the first two years of their marriage and then takes a marble out every time they have sex after that, the jar will never be emptied. First, I don't believe this is generally true, but even where it is true, I find it to be particularly sad.

At one conference where I was speaking, I was seated at a table with—hold your breath—*six* Christian sexual therapists. Their reasoned consensus was that marital sex takes twenty years to reach its peak, at which point it can be more enjoyable than ever. To pursue this, however, you're going to have to grow as a couple in many areas that aren't easy to grow in. Keeping this aspect of marriage alive and fulfilling long-term is, in fact, one of the great challenges of marriage but also one of the most thrilling. It is beyond wonderful to so desire someone you know so well and love so dearly and with whom you have so many pleasant memories.

If you don't reinvent your sexual relationship, intentionally and purposefully, it's going to fade.

The difficulty of maintaining long-term sexual interest can actually be a blessing. Achieving lifelong sexual satisfaction will all but force you to develop the same relational skills that will serve all aspects of marriage: You're going to have to be humble, hear hard words, and learn to put someone else's needs first. You're going to have to learn to understand who your partner is and what he or she truly desires (and doesn't desire). You'll need plenty of courage, as it's easier to just stay quiet in this area than to pursue true intimacy, to be as naked in your conversation and desires as you are in each other's arms. You will have to grow in empathy and patience and generosity.

That's why I believe it is a mark of God's kindness that it can be so difficult to maintain long-term sexual intimacy in marriage after the initial chemistry has faded because it forces us to develop the very skills needed for a marriage to succeed on all levels. If you grow in humility, if you learn how to listen, if you develop courage to bring something up instead of keeping silent, and if you create a marital climate where even the potentially embarrassing realities of "naked" life can be looked at under a microscope, there isn't an element of your marriage that won't benefit from these newly enhanced relational skills.

Lego Sets

Dr. Juli Slattery uses an analogy that is spot-on accurate. Long-term marital sexuality is more like a Lego set than a Tonka truck. A Tonka truck comes out of the box ready to be played with, but Legos are entirely different—the fun is in putting something together. After you build something, however, it's not that much fun for very long. You might enjoy building a Lego boat, but who wants to play with a Lego boat for more than five minutes? So you tear it apart and build something else.

In the same way, to maintain lifelong sexual enjoyment, we have to build, tear down, and rebuild our sexual relationships with our spouses. Sex is one thing when you're newlyweds and alone at home. It changes after it becomes routine and you've become familiar with each other. It's another challenge altogether when kids enter the picture, and you deal with pregnancy, nursing, and the exhaustion of having your sleep schedules blown up. It changes yet again when those kids become toddlers, then teenagers, and then when your bodies begin to age.

In any one of these seasons it is easy to give up. If you've built a sex life that "worked" when you were newlyweds, it's not necessarily going to work with two toddlers and a baby at home. And it would most likely be a disaster when you hit your sixties. If you don't reinvent your sexual relationship, intentionally and purposefully, it's going to fade. The canary is going to die.

I don't want to get too theoretical at the expense of being practical, however, so let's discuss some of the very "physical" aspects of marital sexual intimacy. When we understand how our bodies (and our brains) function, we can better understand the promise, delight, and purpose of sexual intimacy and its role in a lifelong marriage.

Sexual Windows

Oxytocin is a neurochemical that creates feelings of bonding, warmth, and affection. Wives, your husbands likely walk around with quite a bit less oxytocin than you do. If a woman has a high level of oxytocin and the man she's married to has a below-average amount, the difference can be a factor of *ten*. Since oxytocin serves a relationship by providing increased levels of trust and emotional availability (in some circles oxytocin has been used to treat autism), the oxytocin gap between husband and wife can be a problem. Fortunately, God has provided a way to create a natural boost in the husband's brain: the one time that a man's level of oxytocin is most likely to approach that of his wife's is immediately following sexual climax.

Women, why do your husbands want to have sex with you as often as they do (whether they realize this or not)?* Because they may never feel closer to you than immediately following sexual

---

* Certainly, many guys are driven by lust, not a desire to feel closer to their wives, but that's a different discussion. Let's focus here on God's creational intent.

intimacy. Remember—this is by God's design. Because wives already have more elevated levels of oxytocin, they may not notice the uptick after sex as much as men do. If you're already mostly full, eating a sandwich doesn't make you feel that much better. However, if you're super hungry, even that very first bite makes your brain go, "Wow!"

Now, add to the absence of a man's oxytocin the presence of sexual hormones and the general effect of testosterone. Dr. Louann Brizendine, who studied at Yale and Harvard and is now on the faculty of UCSF Medical Center, states, "Men have two and a half times the brain space devoted to sexual drive in their hypothalamus. Sexual thoughts flicker in the background of a man's visual cortex all day and night, making him always at the ready for seizing sexual opportunity."[1] (That said, *many* couples are comprised of a wife with a higher libido than her husband.)

This "stew" creates a situation such that when a man moves past what we could call his "sexual window," his sexual desire can become virtually an obsession. Breasts seem to appear out of nowhere, like magnets to his eyes. He notices a pair of legs in a way he wouldn't have a day or two ago. A provocative advertisement yanks his attention with a force that can startle him.

Every man has a different sexual window, and these windows can certainly change with age. For your husband, the window might be twenty-four hours, seventy-two hours, or a week. But if he's pushed past that window, and you're not available, sexual desire can feel like a freight train pulling him away from you and toward something—or someone—else.

When sexual desire is met in marriage, that window is wonderfully reset. Lust will still be a battle for most men, but it's the difference between saying no to a dessert after having eaten a full meal and turning down a burger when you haven't eaten in three days. It's a different fight altogether.

And here's the payoff, for both of you: By meeting that desire, you release all kinds of very positive oxytocin in your husband's brain, and he bonds with you all over again. He learns to trust you—he was vulnerable, and you didn't use that against him. He learns to treasure you—he needed you, and you were there for him. He learns to appreciate you—he has an intense desire that feels like it could rule him, but that desire dissipates in your arms, with an aftermath that feels like the garden of Eden instead of a guilt-ridden jaunt through accusatory hell.

And women, sexual intimacy leads you into the garden of Eden as well. The woman in Song of Songs 1:2 proclaims that making love with her husband "is more delightful than wine." This book of the Bible speaks of the pleasure a wife gets from sex before it ever addresses the husband's pleasure. God's will for you to enjoy sexual intimacy is further seen in the fact that He designed you with one particular body part that is there for the singular purpose of sexual pleasure. You were designed and created to enjoy sexual intimacy— not merely as a way to satisfy your husband and certainly not just to keep him from sinning, but to relish the act as much, if not more, than he does.

My colleague Sheila Gregoire has a great take on helping couples overcome the arguments about frequency of sexual intimacy. I've heard her say, "Maybe we should stop asking, 'What is the minimum I can get away with?' and start asking, 'How can I make sex a better part of both our lives?' After all, if God made sex to be awesome, why would we want to miss out on that?"

The best strategy, then, isn't to focus on avoiding sin and thus have sex out of fear but, rather, to embrace frequent, mutually shared pleasure that neither of you wants to miss. This book has urged you to embrace a level of selflessness in marriage that is uncommon, but now I'm urging you to embrace the very satisfying ecstasies that are no less God's will for you than appropriate self-denial.

Our sexual desires can either bless our marriages or ruin our integrity. If we ignore them, pretend that they won't drive us or that they can exist without healthy fulfillment, we're being arrogantly foolish. Why try to keep a marriage connected and intimate without utilizing one of the most powerful neurological tools to do just that?

I've sat across from too many couples who felt overly confident about their ability to coast in sexless marriages. Such experiments often end tragically, and that's why they end up sitting in my office with weeping wives and husbands with shame written all over their faces.

God has given us a strong desire (and a command) to keep our marriages together, not to tear them apart, so we need to be intentional about channeling our desires in the right direction—toward each other. If your sexual relationship has crumbled, explore why. Instead of escaping into a substitute like erotica or porn, explore how to overcome the frustrations and disappointments in your own bedroom. You'll never fix your marriage by looking at what's going on in other people's bedrooms!

For some of us, this may mean paying a visit to the doctor to evaluate our physical health. It may mean adjusting our schedules, helping each other out more, or hearing that something we're doing is undercutting our appearance and desirability in the eyes of our spouses. It may also mean being more intentional and thoughtful about meeting our spouses' desires rather than focusing on our own (though ignoring your own desires completely is a short-term strategy that won't serve a lifelong love).

If the canary in your marriage has died, find out what poison killed it and address it. The wonderful thing about the way God designed sexual intimacy for a lifelong marriage is that it can be rediscovered, renewed, and reenjoyed once the "poisons" are removed from the air.

The Depths of Desire

"Talk about world domination!"

My wife had been in a busy season, so I purposefully had planned an evening I knew she would enjoy—dinner at a jazz club followed by an evening of romance. I intentionally let the sexual energy smolder throughout the day. Well before dinnertime, Lisa finally suggested, "Why don't we just get on with it already?" But I simply smiled at her and thought, *Not a chance.*

On the way to the club, I filled up her car's gas tank because I know Lisa hates to fill up her gas tank and she was going to be driving the next day. That may not sound so sexually enticing, but it's not up to us men to determine what constitutes foreplay. Trust me, men, a gesture like that can do wonders; it builds the mood. It makes your wife think, *He's taking care of me.* A spiritually healthy wife who feels taken care of is predisposed to take care of you.

The "dinner"—iceberg lettuce masquerading as a salad, poorly cooked chicken covered with gravy, and *instant* mashed potatoes—was a disaster, given Lisa's organic bent, but she loved the music and atmosphere. It's not a place I would have visited on my own. Lisa knew we were there because of her.

My small physical touches during the dinner were intentional and deliberate but nothing scandalous. If someone from our church had been sitting right behind us, they wouldn't have even noticed. But I've been married to Lisa for more than thirty years and pretty much know how, even in public, I can slowly bring her near to boiling with touches and caresses that no one watching could possibly take offense to or even know what was going on. After three decades of enjoying each other, an innocent-looking caress, a simple touch, a slight moving of her hair can bring to mind past memories and a future promise packed with impending pleasure.

When we got home, I knew what I was going to do, and I did it. It wasn't anything grand, just intentional and thoughtful, and it showed a little preparation. Within minutes Lisa was lying back saying, "Talk about world domination!"

What she meant was "You have conquered me. Do what you will."

When it first came out, the *Fifty Shades of Grey* trilogy was discussed by more marital and Christian bloggers than could be counted, so let me just say this: men, if you need handcuffs and ropes to make your wife feel the enticement of full surrender, you might be doing it wrong.

Try studying her, getting to know her moods and total body—not just the most popular three areas of feminine anatomy, but everything.

Try kindness on a daily basis.

Try spiritual connection—make sure she knows she's supported in prayer.

Try years of giving pleasure unselfishly so that she knows, once things get started, she's going to be carried away by your touches, not used by your demands.

Try taking care of her kids to take care of her.

Try thinking about how you're going to exceed her expectations. It's stunning to think how good we can make our wives feel. Now compare that to how awful it is to leave them unsatisfied because we are focusing on our own pleasure.

If you study your wife and then apply all this, you'll come to a place where you never need handcuffs. What you've got is much stronger, more powerful, more exciting, and more fulfilling—a lifelong love of kept promises and generous service.

My wife's take is that a woman would be less inclined to read about sex with an imaginary billionaire if she were fully enjoying real sex with a thoughtful (and much less wealthy) husband. She's not saying that if a wife is reading erotic novels that her husband is a poor lover—just that it might be a symptom that things have started to slide in the bedroom. "I don't think most women want pain or the kind of sex described in those books," Lisa told me. "I just think they want something a little more creative than what they're getting."

Men, God has given us the capacity to use our bodies to take our wives to places of transcendent pleasure. We can make our wives forget, for a few blessed moments, that they are moms who need to wipe noses and change diapers. They can forget that they're bosses with lazy employees, or employees with buffoon bosses. They can forget there's a house to clean or a doctor's appointment to keep or a car to vacuum or a sick friend to call. They can be transported to a divine place of sighs and holy pleasure and laughter and delight, and when it's all done, we will feel closer to them than ever before.

Only God could make something like this possible.

Long-term sexual satisfaction in marriage requires that we go well beyond gimmicks. If you want to use a gimmick now and then, fine—it's your marriage. But if you think something like that is going to sustain you both through the years, you're fooling yourself.

For long-term satisfaction, you need to study your wife (or husband), not just a few parts of her body. Build years of trust with kind touching and generous pleasuring. Let her know that if she lets herself go in your hands, you'll make her momentarily forget everything bad going on in her life and feel everything good. If you can't get her excited in public, fully clothed, if you need to get her "naked and handcuffed" to feel like things are getting hot, you probably don't know her well enough yet.

Let me add that I know many men have done all of the above and more and yet remain frustrated by the lack of sexual intimacy in their marriages. I've seen levels of bitterness and resentment rise to terrifying heights when a man (and in many cases, a woman) lives with this, and the last thing you need is a pastor telling you that the reason you're not having success is because you're doing something wrong. It's possible you're married to a selfish, narcissistic, or lazy spouse. My counsel is this: bitterness and resentment have never solved a single marital frustration nor made any marital problem go away. Take the energy you're wasting on fretting and instead work with a counselor to find how best to address this situation. If your spouse refuses to see one with you, go by yourself to first learn how to help your spouse understand why this aspect of your marriage needs to be addressed.

It's perfectly holy and God-honoring to think about how to sexually please and thrill your spouse. God knows His daughters and sons work hard and live in a world that neglects them. Do you think He has a problem with us cherishing them, desiring them (and healing their souls in the process), and then releasing in them what God designed for their good—a supremely enjoyable climax? Not a chance. Frankly, I'm of the opinion that God likely wishes we'd have far *more* sex, not less.

What will create and sustain such sexual desire through the years, given the fact that we are sinful people married to other sinful people? *Everything we've talked about in this book.* Literally every chapter, if applied, can improve your sex life.

In a previous chapter we defined true love as a "shared experience of God living in us and God's love being made complete in us." Sex showcases this; it doesn't compete with it. There's a reason so many commentators used to read the Song of Songs as a type of our passionate desire for God.

Sexual desire isn't a problem, as I used to foolishly think. Properly directed, it's a blessing. But a lifelong love doesn't exist on desire alone; it's the other way around. Love sustains the desire; desire doesn't sustain the love. If I truly love my wife outside the bedroom, I will crave her touch between the sheets, and she will crave mine. If I must feel desire before I love, my sexuality and my attitudes will be as spotty as the weather—hot one day and cold the next.

A pastor once told me a moving story about watching an elderly man die and his widow saying good-bye to the man's body. She touched his face, his shoulder, his hands, his legs, and his feet. She was saying good-bye to a body she knew well, a body that had loved her, protected her, served her, and delighted her.

Let's make this our marital legacy. There is a spiritual brilliance to marital love, but if that "spiritual" brilliance neglects physical realities, we're settling for far less than God's best. Keeping "love" in the forefront of your mind whenever you think about or engage in sex with your spouse is the "north star" of sexual satisfaction on all levels.

Building a Lifelong Love

1. Has your sexual relationship with each other brought more healing than hurt? Why do you think that is so? What do you need to do to grow as a couple in this area in the future?

2. Talk with your spouse about one or two times when you felt the pleasure of sexual intimacy with each other at its most intense. What was happening? What set it up? What does this tell you about your relationship and how to build desire in the future?

3. As a wife, do you know what your husband's sexual window is? As a husband, do you know how often your wife feels fulfilled in the bedroom?

4. Be bold and tell your spouse what will most serve you sexually in this season of marriage. Discuss how both of you can best express your love for and appreciation of each other through sexual intimacy.

15

Living Is Giving

A man who heard me speak on marriage decided to apply my suggestion that men use every act of sexual temptation as an opportunity to actively do something for their wives. One of the best ways for husbands to fight lust for other women is to be consumed with loving their wives. We will go much further focusing on loving extravagantly rather than on not falling. Fight sin with love. Use temptation as a reminder to pay attention to your marriage rather than to indulge the possibility of stepping into sin.

In this case, the advice served the man well. He arrived home from work earlier than usual, and his wife was gone. Normally, this would have been a time when the temptation to look at pornography became intense. Remembering what I had said, he decided to take on a chore that his wife normally did: he mowed the lawn.

When his wife arrived home and saw him putting away the lawnmower, she was shocked. "What's going on?" she asked.

"Nothing. I just got home early and saw that the lawn hadn't been mowed. I figured you were busy and thought I'd help you out."

She hugged him like she meant it—maybe for the first time in weeks.

"I can't believe how much difference it made just doing that one simple thing," he told me.

The most telling sign of a true disciple is that we are transformed from selfish people who live for our own pleasure and comfort into disciples who are dedicated to serving others. "Though I am free and belong to no one, I have made myself a slave to everyone, to win as many as possible" (1 Cor. 9:19).

The mark of Jesus is the mark of a giver. His greatest love was seen in giving His life for others. There is no love greater (see John 15:13).

If Jesus truly lives in us, we will delight in giving. We will look for opportunities to give and never grow tired of giving: "Let us not become weary in doing good, for at the proper time we will reap a harvest if we do not give up. Therefore, as we have opportunity, let us do good to all people, especially to those who belong to the family of believers" (Gal. 6:9–10).

Two women wrote a remarkable daily devotional that became a huge bestseller in the early half of the twentieth century. They sensed God telling them:

> Give abundantly. Feel that you are rich. Have no mean thought in your heart. Of Love, of thought, of all you have, give, give, give. You are followers of the World's Greatest Giver. Give of time, of personal ease and comfort, of rest, of fame, of healing, of power, of sympathy, of all these and many more. Learn this lesson, and you will become a great power to help others and to do mighty things.[1]

Is there any calling in life that teaches us to "give, give, give" quite like marriage and parenting? This is a training ground for what it means to be ruled by our Lord Jesus, the chief Giver, who gives us His Holy Spirit, who compels and empowers us to give without limit.

We've got to peel off our selfishness. It's filthy and wet and will make us sick. God wants us to peel it off and be washed and clothed in His *giving* Spirit.

In Jesus' economy, giving is better than receiving (see Acts 20:35). Will you let God use your spouse and your family to help you cherish giving? Will you embrace a life of giving? Will you thank Him for providing an arena in which you can give so abundantly?

Do Not Withhold Good

Many of us like to define our excellence as spouses by what we *don't* do: *I don't get rough with my spouse. I don't gossip about my spouse. I don't yell at my spouse. I don't cheat on my spouse.* But Proverbs 3:27 tells us that excellence is found in what we *do* do, not just what we avoid: "Do not withhold good from those to whom it is due, when it is in your power to act." If you have the opportunity to bless your spouse while possessing the ability to do it but out of laziness or malice you choose not to act, you're in direct violation of this teaching.

If my wife needs to talk and I have the power to listen to her but fail to do so, according to Proverbs 3:27, that's a problem. If I know my spouse needs to be encouraged, but I'm too busy to notice or too apathetic to find a creative way to build her up, that's a problem. If my spouse thinks our sexual relationship is running on fumes, and I can't marshal the energy to revitalize it, that's a problem. If our finances are causing my spouse tremendous stress and I don't step in to better manage it by increasing income and/or curtailing expenses, I'm failing in love.

Instead of saying, "I'm an excellent spouse because I don't do *x*, *y*, or *z*," how about going a step further and saying, "Because I want to be an excellent spouse, today I'm going to do *a*, *b*, and *c*"?

What good are you able to do for your spouse but aren't doing for whatever reason? It doesn't have to be something that would qualify as a sin of omission if you didn't do it. Think a little deeper about things that you know would bless your spouse, that you have the power to do, but for whatever reason you're not doing them. Begin to adopt a *giving* view of marriage.

Slow and Steady, Not Big and Sweaty

My friend Kevin Harney was at a Promise Keepers conference years ago when the speaker asked every man to make a commitment to love his wife in a very practical way when he got home. Some men said they were going to wash their wives' cars. Another said he'd be sure to pick up his socks. One said he'd finally get around to installing some new program on his wife's computer.

Kevin prayed before he answered, and he sensed God asking him, "What does Sherry hate doing the most?"

That was easy: making the bed.

Fine, Kevin thought, *when I get home, I'll make the bed for the next five days.*

"That's not what I meant," God seemed to reply. "Why not do it *every* day, and when you do it, pray for her?"

God was asking Kevin to make a lifetime commitment, which Kevin has kept. He is approaching six thousand times of making the bed while praying for his wife. He even does this when he's at a hotel because he doesn't want to miss the chance to pray for his wife.

Intimate marriage isn't built on the big moments, such as an over-the-top proposal or hitting it out of the park on a birthday or anniversary. Those can be fun times, but the divorce court is littered with marriages that enjoyed occasional parties amid a wasteland of otherwise persistent apathy.

To truly grow your love, it's better to start small and be consistent rather than try to rescue things with a grand gesture. When you notice a malaise seeping into your marriage, or your partner forces you to notice it with a theatrical display of discontent, it's tempting to think you can fix things with one big act of repentance. The problem is, you can't keep a grand gesture going. It may even set up false expectations for the future, ironically making things worse—when it doesn't keep happening, it serves only to highlight the emptiness before and after.

Small acts of kindness, repeated daily, will usually take a marriage much further than a onetime grandiose act of generosity.

> To truly grow your love, it's better to start small and be consistent rather than try to rescue things with a grand gesture.

For instance, men, if your wife says, "You never notice me," and you take her out to dinner, write out a card with fifty things you appreciate about her, and buy her an extravagant gift, she'll feel appreciated for a few hours. If you then go right back to your usual routine, thinking you've taken care of the problem, you'll probably be worse off seventy-two hours later. She'll resent that you seemed to "get it" but now are deliberately *not* getting it anymore.

On the other hand, if you decide you'll take some time to notice your wife for *fifty days in a row*, mentioning one new thing each day and perhaps following up with a small gesture of kindness four or five days a week, you'll get much further with your wife than a single event could ever accomplish. You will also find that it produces a change within yourself that a single grand gesture could not.

Women, if your husband seems starved for sexual affection, and you think one special night in a hotel where you plan, primp, and surprise him with your initiative will satisfy him for a while, you're sadly mistaken. Such a gesture more likely will increase his appetite for more, which will make him notice its absence more. Far better to be consistent in showing sexual love on a weekly basis than to think one grand gesture will make things better.

Small and steady will usually get you further than "big and sweaty."

"You Had Me at Jell-O"

My friends Paul and Virginia Friesen watched a friend's thirty-eight-year-old marriage come to a sad and painful end due to cancer. By Wendy's own description, she and John had shared a "sweet marriage." Part of that sweet marriage involved flying to Hawaii twice each year, and the islands held many special memories of their life together. The first time she went back to Hawaii without John, Wendy asked Paul and Virginia to come along. She couldn't bear to be alone this first time.

As the three of them shared a lunch out on the balcony overlooking the Pacific, Wendy started to cry.

"What is it, Wendy?" Paul asked.

To his surprise, Wendy blurted out, "I wish I'd made him more Jell-O!"

Jell-O?

Her husband's gone and she's thinking about *Jell-O*?

I'll let Paul and Virginia explain:

> Wendy then told us, through laughter and tears, that John loved Jell-O. From the earliest days of their marriage, John always was asking her to make him Jell-O. She didn't like Jell-O herself and declined to make it most of the time, claiming it was all empty calories, nothing but sugar and colored dyes. But now, looking back, she mused, "Why didn't I just give him Jell-O?" As we continued to talk, she said, "The real reason was not all the nutritional stuff, but just that I plain didn't want to make him Jell-O. I didn't like it. But what a simple thing for me to do to bring him a little extra joy for the day. I wish I had made him more Jell-O."

When you look back on your marriage, what will be your "Jell-O," that silly little thing that you denied your spouse? Paul and Virginia go on to say:

> It is my deep conviction that we truly are designed to be at our best when we put our spouses' needs above our own. The irony is that when we do, we actually find the intimacy we have been longing for.... Just as Wendy wished she'd made John more Jell-O, at some point in life, each of us will look back and reflect on our marriage and what could have made it more what we desired and what God designed it to be.[2]

What's your spouse's Jell-O?

Secret Service

One final thought is the biblical notion of doing our good deeds in secret. Marriage must involve obvious acts of love and service, of course, but I believe a truly sacred marriage, with a spouse's hope set on the judgment day, will also include many moments of "secret service" in which we do things for our spouses that they will not recognize or even know about.

As a young husband, I was a master at doing something I knew Lisa would love—one of her love languages could best be described as "acts of cleaning"—five minutes before she was due home. I wanted to be caught in the act and get noticed.

I've grown a bit since then. Fulfilling Lisa's other love language ("not having to fill up my own gas tank") has become a regular part of my life. If I'm leaving on a trip, I make sure her tank is full enough that she won't have to visit a gas station while I'm away. After we bought a new car for her, I made it a game to see how long we could go without her ever having to fill up her own tank. This has become so common that when someone asked Lisa about it she confessed, "I don't really notice anymore. I just don't bother to look at the gas gauge because Gary keeps it pretty full."

Even if Lisa doesn't notice anymore, God does. And caring for her in a way that might not be acknowledged grows my own heart. Doing things for Lisa makes me love her all the more. Lisa told someone recently, "Gary gets so much pleasure out of doing things for me," and that's true. It's one of the most extraordinary changes in my heart since getting married thirty-five years ago—the sheer joy I take in doing something for my wife (and others, for that matter). When we first got married, I may have been the most selfish husband alive.

We *can* grow in both our ability and our desire to love. And getting pleasure out of giving is much more enjoyable than selfish frustration and resentment over what we're not receiving.

Intentionally doing acts of secret service is a win-win-win-win strategy. My spouse is served (win #1), and my lust to be noticed and appreciated is crucified (win #2) so that I can grow in the art of true, unselfish love (win #3). Furthermore, Jesus says that when our works are done in secret, we can expect heavenly rewards (win #4).

Take a few moments and consider how you can love your spouse today through an act of secret service. When our marriages are marked by such generous acts of giving, others will see the love of God in us and perhaps even proclaim, "Behold how they love each other!"

Building a Lifelong Love

1. What is your greatest temptation in life right now? Is there a way that serving your spouse in the face of that temptation (rather than indulging in the sin) can help you overcome that temptation?

2. Proverbs 3:27 says, "Do not withhold good from those to whom it is due, when it is in your power to act." Is there any good you are withholding from your spouse? Does your spouse have a "Jell-O," a small pleasure that you could easily provide?

3. What small, daily act (such as Kevin making the bed and praying for his wife) can you begin doing to adopt a "living is giving" mind-set?

4. Pray about a "secret service" you can do in the next month to love your spouse in a way that only God will know what you have done.

Epilogue

If you looked up "lifelong love" in a sermon illustration dictionary, you'd likely find a picture of Jim and Anne Pierson. This couple has been my Halley's Comet for much of my adult life, passing by every few years. I met them in my twenties while working at Care Net; they ran their own ministry with a similar emphasis named Loving and Caring. We'd see each other at conferences and conventions and catch up on each other's lives and ministries. They saw my children grow up and my hair fall out.

When I left Care Net in my thirties to focus on writing and speaking, I was still invited to the conferences, and Jim was a shelter to me. I'm an insecure introvert called to an extrovert's job, and Jim was a solid place of refuge between sessions. Anne was always such an encouraging presence. She spoke so passionately of how God was using me, in a way I had to believe her despite my insecurities. She had been speaking and writing as her primary vocation for over a decade and served as a wonderful role model.

Jim was a giant of a man. I'm guessing if the scale didn't reach 350 to 400 pounds, it wouldn't be of much use to him. His large girth carried an even larger heart, as he was a dad, pastor, counselor, and mentor to so many people. Though he could be hilarious (I once saw him hold up a hotel-sized bath soap in front of his belly and ask an entire room, "So they think this is going to be enough?"), Jim usually worked behind the scenes. Anne was the teacher, the speaker, and the trainer. Jim ran their book table and kept Anne's life on track.

There was one way, however, that Jim would often steal the spotlight. Before every one of Anne's workshops, just after she was introduced, Jim would slip into the back of the room and belt out the Stevie Wonder tune, "Isn't she lovely? Isn't she wonderful?" The largely feminine audience ate this up, to see a husband affirm his wife so well.

Sadly, Jim had a long and difficult death. He contracted an unusual form of aggressive cancer that, when diagnosed, doctors said would send him home to the Lord within a couple of weeks. Jim hung on for seven months, but they were brutal months sprinkled with some incredible times of ministry. So many people had to cycle through his hospice room to say good-bye that Anne thinks Jim was holding on for their sakes.

The medical costs associated with his end-of-life care would have bankrupted Jim's family if not for the aid of a wealthy business-man whom Jim had led to the Lord. Jim had discipled this man via telephone on a weekly basis for years.

This man said to Anne, "He made me a much better man, a much better father, a much better husband. I want to cover the costs of his care."

"I don't think you realize how much this is going to cost," she protested.

"I don't think you realize how much of an impact Jim has had on my life," the man responded. "Please, let me do this for him."

After Jim finally died, Anne went to her next conference with a heavy heart. Jim had always been there for her, and she had to brace herself to be introduced and not hear Jim break out with his Stevie Wonder song.

Sure enough, the introduction ended, Anne looked up, felt enveloped by the silence, and then apologized. "I'm sorry," she told the crowd, "I just need to pray."

She bowed her head to find strength in God, and when she opened her eyes, someone had placed a flower in a vase right in front of her. Anne was startled, thrown off.

"What's this?" she asked the crowd.

A woman in the front row explained that she had woken up that morning and felt impressed by God that Anne would need something encouraging right before she started speaking. She told her husband to go get a flower in a vase.

"Where am I going to find that?" he asked. "We're not from around here."

"Just get it," she said.

So he did. Anne then told the gathered audience about how Jim had always sung to her before she spoke, how she had dreaded opening her eyes and hearing nothing, and how much that flower meant to her—evidence that God was still with her even though her husband wasn't and that God would see her through.

As you might expect, there was a serious run on Kleenex in that room. And the husband, who admitted that he had protested his wife's request rather vigorously, told Anne, "I'm going to be a different husband. I had no idea how much those small things can really matter."

Jim had discipled another man even *in his death.*

The first time I saw Anne after Jim's passing, I was fighting back tears every fifteen minutes as we remembered her wonderful husband. When she dropped me off at my hotel, she paused to tell me, "I've had such a good life, Gary. Such a good, good life, investing in others and sharing that with Jim."

Though people always spoke so highly of the gifted Anne Pierson, for every time I heard her name in ministry circles, I heard "Jim and Anne Pierson" a dozen times. They had that blessed single identity. They were a unit—two individuals who were very much a single couple.

Jim and Anne had little of what most people think constitutes a glamorous marriage. Having spent their entire married lives in ministry, they had so little money that Jim felt he needed to get permission from Anne to leave his daughter a small gift in his will (less than $10,000) to buy a new car. They didn't look like Angelina Jolie and Brad Pitt. Jim's passing was covered by a local newspaper, but it didn't make the evening news or even *Christianity Today*. But how many people do you know who can look back at a simple but spiritually fruitful life and honestly say, "It's been such a good life, Gary. Such a good, good life, investing in others and sharing that with my husband"?

You don't have to be beautiful—though Jim and Anne were and are, in every way. You don't have to be rich. You don't have to be famous to experience this. You just have to be what Jim and Anne were: worshippers of God, intent on seeking *first* His kingdom and His righteousness, investing in the lives of others, and reaping eternal rewards.

God wants this for you. He wants you to be able to one day say good-bye to your lifelong love with similar words: "It has been such a good, good life, a rich life of investing in others and sharing that with my spouse."

God Hates Domestic Violence

Two days before Christmas, I accidentally sent a decorative reindeer hurtling off a small table in our library. The reindeer shattered into five separate pieces. I picked up each piece, knowing there was no way I could repair this, and presented the evidence to Lisa.

"That's fine," she said, surprising me. "It wasn't that expensive, and I wasn't that into it."

Our passion over the destruction of something is directly related to how important it is to us. On another occasion, I dropped a glass cup that had belonged to Lisa's grandmother. The cup was precious to her. Lisa didn't even have to speak; I could feel the passion.

When will we men understand how precious God's daughters—our wives—are to Him? That to hurt them, to even make them miserable, raises a passion that we can't even imagine? If we don't strive to understand the depths of God's love for our wives, we'll miss the breadth of His wrath when we abuse them. "Since you call on a Father who judges each person's work impartially, live out your time as foreigners here in reverent fear" (1 Pet. 1:17).

The force of a sacred marriage—love, absolute benevolence, living to bless each other and showcase each other, being *for* the other, nurturing each other, encouraging each other—is diametrically opposed to any form of assault. The church should hate domestic violence as much as it hates divorce. When we assume that God hates divorce more than He hates domestic violence, it shows how little we understand His passion for His daughters. It also leads to the disastrous consequence of making women feel like they are obligated to stay in a dangerous situation that God hates. The last thing a woman fleeing a dangerous home should feel is guilt. She is serving God's purpose by ending something He hates—violence against her.

Dallas Willard rightfully broadened the definition of *assault* to other forms of violence that may not be physical: "Merely avoiding domestic violence can still leave the home a hell of cutting remarks, contempt, coldness, and withdrawal or noninvolvement. Such a hell is often found in the homes of Christians and even of Christian leaders."[1] Not all forms of such activity may warrant divorce, but they certainly raise the wrath of God and deserve to be called out every bit as much as God's hatred of divorce.

Pastors, we must hold all forms of marital assault with the same contempt with which God holds it. Sometimes, it seems like we are more concerned with keeping the marriage going than ending the violence, when in reality, violent men need to understand that in order to keep the marriage going, the violence must stop *now*. Notice how we tend to put the onus on the woman instead of the man: "Wife, stay in the marriage" rather than "Husband, we cannot support your wife staying with you as long as you harm her."

We won't counsel like this until we hate domestic violence as much as God hates it. We need to recognize the harm it does to the children, the deplorable witness it gives to the world, the damage it does to a woman's soul (not to mention her body), the corrupting influence it has on the male perpetrator, and especially the pain it causes our heavenly Father-in-Law who hates to see His daughters abused. It is as ugly a sin as you can find.

Would you ever counsel your daughter to stay in a place where she winces when she sees a knife or flinches when her husband touches her? Would you ever tell her to spend a night in a home where she's not entirely sure she'll wake up unbruised or even alive in the morning? Wouldn't you do everything in your power to get her out of there sooner rather than later?

Every Christian wife should be able to look at her husband's hands not as a threat but as a source of provision, tools with which he will work hard for her and her children. She should be able to see his hands not as instruments of pain but as a source of sexual pleasure, tools for loving caresses and cherishing affection. She should be able to see his hands as a source of protection, tools of defense that will take the shape of a fist only to protect the family he loves and never, not even once, to turn on them.

When we think that keeping a marriage together is the only biblical solution, even if it means preserving a violent situation, we have become beholders of legalism and strangers to God's true passion. The destruction of a marriage is a terrible thing, but the destruction of a woman's soul, the damage to the children's psyches, and the triumph of fear and hatred where there should be faith, hope, and love are just as bad.

The last thing I am is "soft" on divorce. I have pleaded with couples to reconcile, and I have stressed that making a poor choice in your twenties doesn't give you an escape clause in your thirties when you meet a "better" choice.

But when I truly understand that my wife is God's daughter—that every believing woman is God's daughter—domestic violence isn't something I just want to "treat." It's something I've learned to hate, as God hates it. And if getting the woman out of the house is the only way to bring it to an end, then the sin is on the man who hurts, not the woman who flees.

When Jesus seemed so hard and so cold to the scribes, when He called them out and sounded nothing less than vicious in His denunciations, what was He angry about? "They that devour widows' houses" (Mark 12:40 ASV).

If we start messing with God's daughters, we're hitting Him where it hurts the most. We're raising the most furious of His passions. We're putting ourselves directly in the line of His red-hot wrath.

My friend Dr. Steve Wilke's contention that marital abuse is "any non-nurturing behavior" may not be the standard for divorce, but it is most definitely the benchmark of every sacred marriage.

I have been told that my book *Sacred Marriage* has been used as an argument for abused women to grit their teeth and bear it. The only one more appalled by this than me is God. I want to leave no misunderstanding about where I stand in this book, and thus I offer this appendix to make it absolutely clear that any form of marital abuse, especially domestic violence, is in direct violation of a lifelong love. It goes against the spirit of every chapter of this book that I offer before God, to you.

Notes

Introduction: It's What You Do with It

1. Joseph Awe, "The Mennonites of Belize—A Brief History," Belize.com, accessed October 22, 2020, https://belize.com/the-mennonites-of-belize-a-brief-history.

Chapter 1: Worshipping Our Way to Happiness

1. Annejet Campbell, comp., *Listen for a Change* (London: Grosvenor, 1986), 90, 93.

Chapter 2: Passion Sustained through Purpose

1. Kevin Miller and Karen Miller, *More Than You and Me: Touching Others through the Strength of Your Marriage* (Colorado Springs: Focus on the Family, 1994), 3.

2. Miller and Miller, *More Than You and Me*, 6.

3. Miller and Miller, *More Than You and Me*, 7.

4. Miller and Miller, *More Than You and Me*, 8.

5. Julie Hatsell Wales, "Letters," *Marriage Partnership*, Winter 1991, 8.

6. Miller and Miller, *More Than You and Me*, introduction.

Chapter 3: Making the Last Things the First Thing Today

1. Jonathan Edwards, "The Christian Pilgrim," in *The Protestant Pulpit: An Anthology of Master Sermons from the Reformation to Our Own Day*, comp. Andrew W. Blackwood (Grand Rapids, MI: Baker Books, 1977), 41.

Chapter 4: The Glory of Spiritual Dependence

1. Rob Rienow and Amy Rienow, *Visionary Marriage: Capture a God-sized Vision for Your Marriage* (Nashville: Randall House, 2010), 19–20.

Chapter 5: A Monk's Marriage

1. Walter Hilton, *The Scale of Perfection,* trans. John P. H. Clark and Rosemary Dorward (New York: Paulist Press, 1991), 244.

Chapter 6: A Marriage Worthy of Our Calling

1. John Stott and Andrew T. LePeau, *Reading Ephesians with John Stott: 11 Weeks for Individuals or Groups*, (Downers Grove, IL: InterVarsity Press, 2017), 85–6.

Part 2: Growing Together

1. Horace Bushnell, "Every Man's Life a Plan of God," in *The Protestant Pulpit: An Anthology of Master Sermons from the Reformation to Our Own Day*, comp. Andrew W. Blackwood (Grand Rapids, MI: Baker Books, 1977), 80.

Chapter 7: Supernatural Science

1. Calum MacLeod, "China Loves Vintage US Cars, Despite Legal Roadblocks," *USA Today*, October 18, 2013, www.usatoday.com/story/news/world/2013/10/18 /china-classic-cars/3001091/.

Chapter 8: Pushing Past the Power Shifts

1. Kayt Sukel, *This Is Your Brain on Sex: The Science Behind the Search for Love* (New York: Simon & Schuster, 2013), 5.

2. Kim Painter, "Moms Really Do Have a Nose for That Baby Smell," *USA Today*, October 2, 2013, 5D.

3. Annejet Campbell, comp., *Listen for a Change* (London: Grosvenor, 1986), 4.

4. The quotes in this section are taken from three sources: a personal lecture and subsequent private conversation with Dr. McQuilkin; and Robertson McQuilkin, *A Promise Kept: The Story of an Unforgettable Love* (Carol Stream, IL: Tyndale, 1998), 3, 13, 18–19, 22, 31–33, 50–53.

Chapter 9: Naked and Unashamed

1. Justin Davis and Trisha Davis, *Beyond Ordinary: When a Good Marriage Just Isn't Good Enough* (Carol Stream, IL: Tyndale, 2013), 59.

Chapter 11: Our Greatest Need

1. Linda Dillow, *What's It Like to Be Married to Me?: And Other Dangerous Questions* (Colorado Springs: David C Cook, 2011), 111–13.

Chapter 14: Delightful Desire

1. Louann Brizendine, *The Male Brain: A Breakthrough Understanding of How Men and Boys Think* (New York: Harmony, 2011), 4.

Chapter 15: Living Is Giving

1. A. J. Russell, ed., *God Calling* (Uhrichsville, OH: Barbour, 2011), August 30 entry.

2. Paul Friesen and Virginia Friesen, *The Marriage App: Unlocking the Irony of Intimacy* (Bedford, MA: Home Improvement Ministries, 2013), 21–22, 167.

Appendix: God Hates Domestic Violence

1. Dallas Willard, *Renovation of the Heart: Putting on the Character of Christ* (Colorado Springs: NavPress, 2012), 190.

Author Information

For information about Gary's speaking schedule, visit his website: www.garythomas.com.

Follow Gary on:
> Twitter (@garyLthomas)
> Facebook (www.facebook.com/authorgarythomas)
> Instagram (garythomasbooks)

To inquire about inviting Gary to your church or community, visit his website (www.garythomas.com) and click on Contact.

Visit Gary's *Closer to Others* blog, where he writes about married life (and singles who want to get married), and *Closer to Christ*, a blog that addresses the deeper Christian life. Both blogs can be found at www.garythomas.com/blog.

Please note that Gary is not able to provide counseling via email or Zoom.

At David C Cook, we equip the local church around the corner and around the globe to make disciples. Come see how we are working together—go to **www.davidccook.org**. Thank you!

transforming lives together

Made in the USA
Las Vegas, NV
15 November 2022

59525579R00132